William Shakespeare
Subject of the Crown?

Tudor and Stuart Sovereignty in Shakespeare's
'Problem-Plays':

The Merchant of Venice
Macbeth
Measure for Measure
The Winter's Tale

Manuela Sonntag M.A.

-Imprint-
Coverdesign: Manuela Sonntag, Christine Klotz,
Portrait reproduction: Wikimedia Commons
Copyright: Manuela Sonntag, 2016
Publisher: BoD – Books on Demand, Norderstedt

ISBN: 9 - 783741 - 242977

Table of Contents

Introduction
Aims and Confinement 8
Methods and Structure 11

The Tudor and Stuart Age
The English Renaissance 14
The Virgin Queen and the English Protestants 22
Mary Stuart and the English Catholics 26
The Elizabethan Age 31
James I and the Union of the Crowns 37
The Dawn of Revolution 41
Elisabeth, James and English Renaissance Theatre 44
The Author Shakespeare 51
Shakespeare and English Monarchy 56

Shakespeare's Plays
The Merchant of Venice 64
    Merchants and Jews 71
    Portia and the Law 77
Macbeth 83
    Macbeth and the Scottish Heredity 91
    Witches and Daemons 102
Measure for Measure 109
    Angelo, the Duke and the Ways of Power 117
    Isabella, the Duke and the Trial Scene 126
The Winter's Tale 134
    Shepherds, Women and Courtiers 143
    Leontes, Perdita and the Golden Age 154

Conclusion 165

Annex 173

Introduction

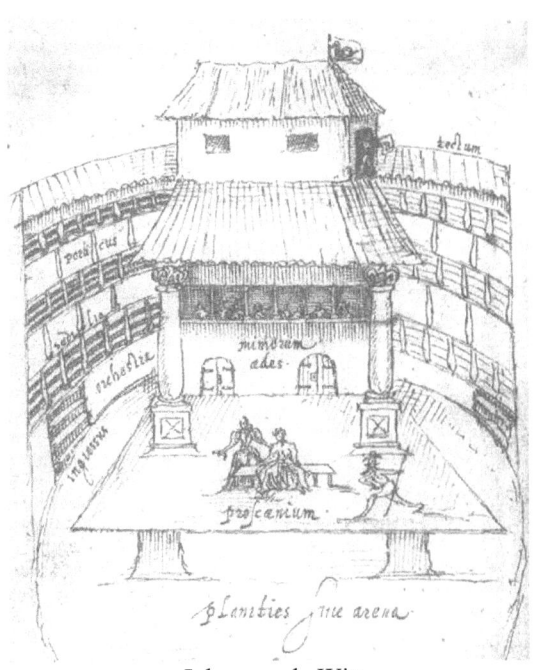

Johannes de Witt
"*A performance in progress at the Swan theatre in London in 1596*"

Aims and Confinement

> *Alone of the major artists of the Renaissance, Shakespeare has no tangible personality outside his art.*[1]

Shakespeare and his work have inspired many books by literary scholars and historians throughout the century. Yet the problem stated above has been an essential part in all of them. What can we know about a man of whom nothing is known, except what he chose to let his characters say and do? Can there really be any certainty about Shakespeare's opinions, thoughts, ideas, even on the most trivial matters? Isn't this a dangerous confusion of person and fiction?

This essay will not try to find certainty among the many statements made about author and work over the years but try to relate some of Shakespeare's 'non-historical' plays to contemporary politics and *[...] by* politics *I refer to those social processes in which relationships of power are conveyed.*[2]

This will therefore be a twofold essay – one part dedicated to the English Renaissance as a century of change and progress, the other part literary analysis of Shakespeare's plays with consideration of this political zeitgeist. Many historians today assume that history does not effectively consist of 'timeless' facts. History is what the majority believes; it is a phenomenon of zeitgeist, propaganda and perception. This development of perception can easily be traced in Shakespeare. Nobody in the English Renaissance would have considered Shakespeare to be anti-Semitic – in fact the term did not even exist - but today productions of *The Merchant of Venice* are to be undertaken with extreme caution and are not considered 'funny' anymore. Scotland's bloody history traced in *Macbeth* causes horror and repulsion in modern audiences, while in Shakespeare's time people were terrified of the evil powers of witches and daemons.

---

[1] Worden, Blair. 2004. "Shakespeare and Politics." In: Alexander, Catherine M. S. (ed.). *Shakespeare and Politics*. Cambridge: Cambridge Univ. Press. pp. 22-44.; pp. 23

[2] Goldberg, Jonathan. 1989. *James I. and the Politics of Literature*. Stanford, CA: Stanford Univ. Press.; pp. XI

This essay will try to find some perceptions of sovereignty and authority in Shakespeare's more problematic plays - *The Merchant of Venice, Macbeth, Measure for Measure* and *The Winter's Tale*. These four plays were chosen for their ambiguous nature that *could* suggest a more serious purpose for their production than mere entertainment.

Many critics can not even agree on whether *The Merchant of Venice* is supposed to be a comedy or a tragedy, but in addition to that it presents a highly interesting trial, a curiously strong female figure and many insights into the world of merchants and trade – a highly important renaissance topic not only for Venice.

Macbeth is not often listed among the problematic plays, but still it stands apart from the other tragedies in the way of presenting its 'hero'. Macbeth and Lady Macbeth are outside the common conception of vice and virtue, acting under the evil supernatural influence of witches – a curious novelty in English renaissance theatre. The 'good' characters are presented only marginally and the fact that all this is based on the half-fictional, half-historical ancestry and the literary works of King James I, makes *Macbeth* highly relevant for the topic of this paper.

Meanwhile, not many critics disagree with the problem-play aspect of *Measure for Measure*. The outspoken sexuality and the interesting blend of 'good' and 'bad' characters are one major aspect of the play. For this paper, however, its most interesting feature is presented in 'The Duke of Venice', who is supposed to be a great believer in contemporary political theory. Here may be a chance to see the author behind the character.

Finally, *The Winter's Tale* also qualifies for both categories of comedy and tragedy. In addition it has a lot to say about abandoned daughters, jealous husbands and the general question of the legitimacy of a ruler – concerning both his ancestry and his ability. This major theme is also considered to be the constant struggle of both the Tudor and Stuart lineage, and it will be interesting to see in which way Shakespeare presents his characters and their opinions.

I will try to work out all those hints and perceptions and try to link them to the 'political persona Shakespeare'. The before mentioned problem of confusing the 'opinion' of a character with the opinion of an author must of course be taken into consideration. A certain proof for Shakespeare's political ambition will not – and cannot – be given in this essay.

In particular, it will focus on finding hints for the following questions:

Was Shakespeare concerned with political developments apart from some minor allusions to entertain the courtiers? Are there allegories criticising or praising the reigning monarch? Is there a possibility that Shakespeare's plays were used as political propaganda? And who would this propaganda have served – the monarch or the opposition?

Method and Structure

Although his plays were well received at Court he did not stoop to flatter the reigning monarch.[3]

The underlying claim for this essay in particular and historical literary criticism in general is the key assumption that no man lives outside his contemporary social and cultural environment. The zeitgeist influence on the evaluation and perception of history mentioned before has been traced throughout Shakespeare's works and set in correlation to the political events of his time. Unlike character traits or personal opinions, this general 'worldview' is much harder to 'conceal' behind the face of a fictional character, for it is assumed that it influences the way *how* a characters acts and speaks and not only *what* it does or says.

This paper will therefore focus on giving, on the one hand, a short survey of Tudor and Stuart history, developments of society, law and government. Beginning with the reign of Henry VIII, England and the 'Crown lands' of Wales and Ireland were given over to a thorough social process of change and progress. The religious crisis and the import of Protestant ideals deeply affected the political and cultural conditions. With the reign of Elizabeth I England experienced a first 'Golden Age' in trade, art and science. Shakespeare arrived in London when this age was already closing and wrote his most famous plays under the reign of James I, but it can be assumed that he was – as were his contemporaries – deeply affected by the so-called 'Elizabethan World Picture' and all emerging consequences.

The shaping of an Elizabethan or Jacobean Drama will be discussed separately, to a more detailed extent, and examined for signs of anti-royalist tendencies in the forerun to the civil-war to see if *Shakespeare's drama presents us with an almost constant interrogation of historical transition, regime change, usurpation and tyranny.*[4]

---

[3] Badawi, M. M. 1981. *Background to Shakespeare.* London: Macmillan Press.; pp. 24

[4] Alexander, Catherine M. S. 2004. "Introduction." In: Alexander, Catherine M. S. (ed.), *Shakespeare and Politics*. Cambridge: Cambridge Univ. Press.; pp. 3

The analysis of the actual plays will provide a short survey of the plot and essential characters, as well as information on the source text and the first known performance. The more detailed analysis will deal with the before mentioned points of historical literary criticism, focussing on the perception of monarchic and religious sovereignty shown by the author. Wherever possible, events and characters will be traced back to historical events described in the first part of the essay, with the confinement mentioned before that a connection can only be suggested and not proven.

The paper will end in a conclusion consisting of a summary trying to give some answers to the questions raised in the introduction and a general consideration of the limits and possibilities that have been encountered and developed in analysing Shakespeare as 'a royal subject'.

Due to the limited frame of this essay, a complete analysis of either the Elizabethan world or the full impact of the examined plays will not be possible: However, if a statement about Shakespeare's political motivation can be given at all, it seems important not to draw any conclusions from a more detailed description of only one play but to collect evidence from repeated incidents and suggestions. It is the author's conviction that Shakespeare, as a man only visible through the contorting mirror of his art, should be glimpsed from as many angles as possible in order to yield a conclusive general picture.

The Tudor and Stuart Age

Elisabeth I of England c.1575
The "Darnley Portrait", National Portrait Gallery, London

The English Renaissance

No other age in English history has brought to light so many aspects for the construction of an English national identity as the age of the Tudors.[5]

The Tudor dynasty ultimately arose from a decade of uncertainty and rebellion. The Wars of the Roses between the two ruling houses of Lancaster and York had brought terror and poverty to most of the English lands. Nevertheless, the rise of the Tudor house was unexpected, Henry Tudor having only an evanescently small claim to the Lancaster lineage. Indeed he was one of the few noble persons in the realm who had almost no claim to the throne at all.[6]

The Tudor line of kings had to trace their legitimacy back to Queen Catherine, a French princess and wife of King Henry V, who was illegally married a second time to her Welsh chamberlain Owen Tudor – the proclaimed kinship to the House of Lancaster did therefore only exist through marriage and neither French nor Welsh nobility was sufficiently respected to support an attempt at kingship. But like many great royal houses the Tudors had mastered the art of political marriage. Thus the son of Queen Catherine, who was not a Lancaster in her own right, was married to Princess Margaret Beauford, who was. The Beaufords were one of the most powerful Lancaster families and provided the support that was needed for Henry VII to finally seize power, both the Lancaster and York clans having lost too many of their princes, after the battle of Bosworth. He then made another clever move in marrying Elisabeth of York. The people of England and Wales were desperate for the civil war to end and their wish for peace became the leading argument for their loyalty to the Tudor house which finally united the 'two roses'.

Nevertheless, the shadow of unrightful kingship remained constantly hovering behind the Tudor ancestry, as did the accusation of bastardy. As mentioned before, these two are the central themes that

---

[5] Esser, Raingard. 2004. *Die Tudors und die Stuarts.* Stuttgart: Kohlhammer Urban.; pp. 15 [translation my own]

[6] Rex, Richard. 2006. *Die Tudors. Englands Aufbruch in die Neuzeit 1485-1603.* Essen: Magnus.; pp. 11

unite the Tudors, the Stuarts and some of Shakespeare's ruling houses.

King Henry's famous son Henry VIII brought new stability by his long and powerful reign and, incidentally, he was never meant to become king. Kingship should have passed to his older brother Arthur, who had married the rich Spanish princess Catherine of Aragon and thereby restored the relationship between the English crown and Habsburg. Only because Prince Arthur died only five months after his wedding, Henry became king of England and only because of the immense dowry of Catherine was he freed by the pope to marry his brother's wife[7] – which would later become the famous *Great Matter*.[8] To include the many aspects of Henry's reign would certainly go beyond the scope of this essay which is supposed to deal with the rulers of Shakespeare's time. There are, however, two developments in the history of Henry VIII that are essential to understand the Elizabethan Age and consequently Shakespeare as well: Church and Succession.

It is often said that Henry VIII broke with Rome because he was madly in love with Anne Boleyn – this reason alone, however, would not have been sufficient for a skilled politician to cause such a disruption with one of the most powerful authorities of that time. In addition, the Roman emperor Charles V was a considerable strength in himself too, and he was closely related to Queen Catherine. The real problem in the king's marriage was succession. It was feared that if the king died without a male heir to suceed him, civil war would inevetably ensue.[9] The terror of a new civil war was still a major fear in Tudor England and the stability of the male Tudor heritage was to be secured at all costs. The only other woman ever to inherit the English throne, Mathila, mother of the later King Henry II, had lead to a dreadful civil war with her cousin Stephen I and thus served only to underline the skeptical view of female rulers in England.[10]

---

[7] Suerbaum, Ulrich. 1989. *Das elisabethanische Zeitalter.* Stuttgart: Reclam.; pp. 70-71

[8] Esser, Raingard; *Die Tudors und die Stuarts*; pp. 41

[9] Maurer, Michael. 1997. *Eine kleine Geschichte Englands.* Stuttgart: Reclam.; pp. 97

[10] Esser, Raingard; *Die Tudors und die Stuarts*; pp. 41

Queen Catherine had not succeeded in that respect, her only surviving child was a daughter and she herself was considered to be beyond fertility. Technically the kings wish would therefore not have been much of a problem, infertility being a common justification for 'divorce' – or rather the pontifical annulment of a marriage. However, the pope was in deep trouble and effectively a hostage of Charles V at that time, who saw his influence on the English policy fading should his aunt be sent back to Spain. This correlation of powers on the continent seemed to have escaped Henry completely, for he was surprised and outraged when the pope sent his refusal of annulment. Henry had used his considerable reputation to support the papal authority against Luther and his adherence. No he believed it was time for the pope to support him in turn.[11]

Until this point his religious doubts concerning his marriage were of no serious political importance, the queen's infertility ought to have been reason enough for judicial purposes. With the pope's refusal, however, a plan evolved that would make the 'King's Conscience' the central point of argument.

In 1521 Henry had been made *defensor fidei* by the Vatican in reward of his treatise against Martin Luther; a little more than ten years later in 1533, when the pope had not grated him his favour in return, the parliament was presented with the *Act in Restrain of Appeals* – an official law persecuting all inhabitants of the British Isles to seek any but the king's judgement in matters of marriage and inheritance. A small concession to the Vatican remained in the exception from questions of heresy, which remained under pontifical judgement for the time being. Archbishop Cramner was instructed to secure the annulment of the king's marriage as soon as possible. It may be disputed if it was a mistake to rush these affairs in such a rude way, for Queen Catherine was as popular in London as Anne Boleyn was not. Her trial and impressing strength of devotion to a husband that had already replaced her caused some uproar on her behalf throughout the country and greatly diminished the king's popularity. However, in the given circumstances there was no way of taking more time over the decisions, because by 1533 Anne Boleyn was pregnant and it was of the utmost importance that her son was born in a legal marriage. In truth, Henry and Anne were secretly married, so suddenly and with so few witnesses that the legitimacy

---

[11] Rex, Richard; *Die Tudors. Englands Aufbruch in die Neuzeit 1485-1603.*; pp. 62

of their bond was in question from the start and the Vatican officially anathematised Henry as a result. This decision washed away all compromises and religious concerns that may have been left in the king and in 1534 the parliament officially passed his *Act of Submission of the Clergy* and the *Act of Supremacy*. For the monarchy itself the rupture with Rome resulted in a tremendous gain of power. The Act of Supremacy made Henry a god-given ruler, who had to fear no other authority over him – other than God's of course.[12]

All decisions concerning the English church were now under supreme rule of the king – the substitution of bishops, the persecution of heresy and the charge of tributes. But the fear of revolution and rebellion was a central feature in the reigns after the civil war and therefore the king insisted that all his courtiers and counsellors had to take a vow onto the *Act of Supremacy*, insuring their loyalty to the king as Head of Church. 45 members of court refused and were consequently put to death on charge of high treason – most notably among them the former Lord Chancellor and noted author Thomas More. The reckless rooting-out of opposition is another feature often seen in Shakespeare too.

In the Elizabethan Age, the breach with Rome gave rise to a special pride in national identity, evolving from Roman and Norman backgrounds rather than continental Christian history.[13] The problem of succession, however, remained unsolved after Queen Anne gave birth to only another daughter – Elisabeth. Henry's older daughter Mary had been proclaimed illegitimate when his marriage with Catherine was annulled so the *status quo* was unchanged; the king was still the father of only one legitimate daughter. After another pregnancy that ended in a miscarriage in 1535, Anne was beheaded under charge of adultery and high treason in 1536. She was tried by a tribunal of 22 peers but only her musician, who was submitted to torture, confessed to the crime.

It has to be said however that the surviving documents used in the trial show that the charces were supported with flimsy and in parts obviously fabricated evidence. If there ever was a true ground for the accusations can therefore not be determined today.[14]

---

[12] Esser, Raingard; *Die Tudors und die Stuarts*; pp. 45

[13] Suerbaum, Ulrich; *Das elisabethanische Zeitalter*; pp. 521

[14] *Suerbaum, Ulrich; Das elisabethanische Zeitalter*; pp. 89

The king married again in secret and Anne Boleyn's daughter was declared illegitimate, just like her half-sister.

King Henry VIII was clearly one of the most impressive rulers of his century. He laid out the concept for the Anglican Church, the Privy Council, the English Bible and the practise of parliamentary legislation.[15] The story of the king's wives and his desperate attempts on securing the stability of the Tudor lineage meanwhile have filled many books already and are no further topic of this essay. It remains to constitute that at the end of his life and in his sixth marriage he had still 'achieved' just one surviving son, who was only nine years old by the time his father died, and two illegitimate daughters no one really considered as heirs to the throne. His last *Act of Succession* in 1546 nevertheless listed them in second and third place and left detailed instructions for the formation of a privy council for the young king Edward VI. Most of his testament, however, was 'reinterpreted' after his death, which gave way to what is sometimes called the *Mid-Tudor Crisis*.[16]

Whereas Edward's rule, as in the case of most regencies, led to fierce power struggels between the leading nobles of his court, his sister Mary's reign remains overshadowed by the often brutal re-introduction of the catholic faith she instigated.[17] The reign of King Edward VI was in some respects even more insignificant than that of his older sister Mary. He was constantly overshadowed by the great lords that proclaimed themselves Lord Protector – Somerset and Northumberland. Nevertheless, he succeeded in strengthening the Protestant aspect of the Anglican Church, which was in the conception of Henry VIII mainly Catholic without yielding to the Vatican. In 1549, Archbishop Cramner was allowed to publish the first *Book of Common Prayer* which was supported by the *Act of Uniformity* – the attempt of installing one prayer book, one dogma and one belief in England. Later, in 1552, both book and law were given over to an even more thorough Protestant revision, forbidding for example the performance of requiems, liturgical vestments and religious idols. These religious matters seemed to be of more importance to the young king than the struggles and revolts of the

---

[15] Rex, Richard; *Die Tudors. Englands Aufbruch in die Neuzeit 1485-1603.*; pp. 48

[16] Maurer, Michael; *Eine kleine Geschichte Englands*; pp. 114

[17] Esser, Raingard; *Die Tudors und die Stuarts*; pp. 60

English nobility. He had to put to death two of his uncles under charge of high treason. The Lord Admiral Thomas Seymour had tried to overpower his almighty brother, the Lord Protector, by marrying the king's widow Catherine Parr and trying to take Edward hostage. But the Lord Protector's position was crumbling from within as his cabinet was unable to cope with the vast inflation, the unstoppable increase of population, years of war expenses in Scotland and France and crop failures in England.

Thus the threat of revolts among the poor or social uheavel in the city of London grew steadily.[18] The fall of the Lord Protector was imminent when his successor Northumberland achieved a bloody but total defeat of the rebellions in East Anglia 1549. In 1551, Somerset was sentenced to death after a half-hearted attempt on rebellion and two years imprisonment.

The king's death, however, offers the really interesting perspective on English history. In awareness of his illness and with the prospect of handing his crown to his crypto-Catholic sister Mary, he tried to change the *Act of Succession* laid out by his father and to make his cousin Jane Grey queen instead. He would naturally have preferred to pass kingship to his promising Protestant sister Elisabeth, however, he could not proclaim Mary illegitimate without ruling out Elisabeth as well – both their mothers' marriages were annulled by common law. It can be assumed that the plan covering this dilemma was greatly influenced by Northumberland, who had readily married one of his sons to the queen-to-be, but it turned out to be a desperate attempt. Mary was forewarned of her planned imprisonment, while the death of King Edward was being kept secret, and escaped to Suffolk. There she quickly found more than 2000 followers to march against Northumberland. Despite of her Catholic conviction and her sex, the loyalty towards the Tudor house was so overpowering that Northumberland's troops deserted almost immediately.

Indeed the respect for the Tudor succession remained significant enough to bring Mary Tudor to the throne, despite her catholic faith and her string bonds to Spain, which were frowned upon by her council.[19] Also for some surely the succession of Queen Mary I was a ray of light in the strict, pre-puritan, Protestant court of King Edward. Had Edward survived and been able to pursue his puritan

---

[18] Maurer, Michael; *Eine kleine Geschichte Englands*; pp. 117

[19] Maurer, Michael; *Eine kleine Geschichte Englands*; pp. 123

ideals, maybe there would have been no court entertainments, no anglican church musik, no theaters and no Shakespeare plays today.[20] It is of course idle to discuss whether Queen Mary was the saviour of art and music in the Tudor lineage, but it must be said that her plans for a return to Catholicism did not meet with the opposition expected from a wholeheartedly Protestant country. Of course, the more outspoken Protestant privy counsellors were banned and replaced with trustworthy representatives of the 'Old Faith'. But for the common people it still made little difference whether they listened to the service in Latin or English. The first serious drop in popularity emerged instead from the queen's *Spanish Marriage*.[21] It was a woman's foremost duty to marry and bear children, and for a queen there could be even less doubt about that. Still, Mary's choice of Prince Phillip, who was to be Phillip II of Spain before long, caused a serious uproar among the population. As the second most important duty of a woman was loyalty and obedience to her husband, the English peers and gentry feared the imminent influence of Habsburg on queen and country. In the year 1544, when Mary was desperately awaiting her husband, the *Wyatt Rebellion* marched against London and for the first time in living memory a revolution army reached the capital.[22] The rebellion marched in the name – but not with the assistance – of Princess Elisabeth, which nevertheless lead to her imprisonment. 'Queen' Jane and her husband where charged with high treason and beheaded and some of Mary's counsellors tried to persuade her that her sister was a threat to the succession of her children. Yet Mary decided to leave her sister in custody and gained her title 'Bloody Mary' elsewhere.

Many historians agree that the reign of Queen Mary I was a catastrophe. Only in recent years efforts are made to explain – if not to justify – her political decisions. Mostly she behaved like a good Catholic and wife, but unfortunately not like a good ruler. Her support for Phillip's war against France lost England his long-time continental beachhead Calais. In her devotion to purify the country from Protestant heresy almost 300 men and women were burnt alive at the stake, among them some of the most able thinkers of the time, like Cramner and Latimer.

---

[20] Rex, Richard; *Die Tudors. Englands Aufbruch in die Neuzeit 1485-1603.*; pp. 137
[21] Suerbaum, Ulrich; *Das elisabethanische Zeitalter;* pp. 102
[22] Suerbaum, Ulrich; *Das elisabethanische Zeitalter;* pp. 103

It is perhaps no coincidence that Channel 5 included Mary Tudor in a series labelled *The Most Evil Men and Women in History*, which aired in time for the golden jubilee of Queen Elisabeth II.[23] Today some more differentiated accounts stress the stability of succession, the attempts on stopping inflation and the queen's devotion to her people. Still, good intentions count for very little in the ruling of a country – as will be seen in *Macbeth* – and it must be concluded that Mary was unsuccessful in all her attempts – she could not produce a catholic heir and her hopes that her sister Elisabeth would continue her catholic agenda prooved naive.[24]

Still, Queen Mary I perhaps has had more influence on Elizabethan policy as was acknowledged for a long time. She – like Elisabeth – had been Princess of Wales in her childhood, but unlike Edward or Elisabeth nobody had given her what could be called a political education. Then she was – again like her sister – declared a bastard, sent away from court, humiliated and ignored for a very long time.

Her reign is largely associated with terror, religious oppression and the fear of foreign rule, because of her desperate marriage. Her sister Elisabeth was forced to witness all of these failures and wrong decisions and tried to avoid them rigorously. And most importantly, Mary's reign smoothed the way for Queen Elisabeth's succession, for in the nine days of Queen Jane it had become obvious that the people of England would rather face a female Tudor on the throne than allow a new outbreak of war among the nobility.

---

[23] Esser, Raingard; *Die Tudors und die Stuarts*; pp. 67
[24] Esser, Raingard; *Die Tudors und die Stuarts*, pp. 67

The Virgin Queen and the English Protestants

She was a natural-born queen as her sister had never been – the most masculine of all female sovereigns in history.[25]

That Elisabeth I should one day be famous because of the mystical quality of her virginity was not to be expected when she became queen in 1558. Many plots – the Wyatt Rebellion among them – had used her name in connection to one aristocrat or another in order to present an alternative to Mary's reign and the Spanish domination. Elisabeth promised to be an able and strong ruler; she had been well educated and shown considerable political tact during the Wyatt affair. She was also adept in financial matters, her means having been very limited throughout her youth, and showed considerable skill in image policy. In later years her summer passages through the country would be celebrated like folk festivals, providing her with huge popularity, but being paid for by her noble hosts. Yet her childhood had suffered like her sister Mary's from the constant uncertainty of her position. She was declared a bastard by her own father, reinstated into heritage in 1546, favoured by her brother in his days of power, declared a bastard again in his attempt to secure the Protestant religion and she had suffered humiliation, imprisonment and constant threats from Mary's counsellors. Her true legal position was not to be proven, for the reopening of her mother's case was out of question. She compromised by emphasizing her strong resemblance to her father and hurried to form a trustworthy cabinet, reducing the number of Mary's privy counsellors from more than 50 to only a dozen. She could not, however, issue any proclaimation to clear up the chaos of Henry VIII marital maneuvers without endangering her own position as heir to the throne.[26]

---

[25] G.R. Elton as quoted in: Suerbaum, Ulrich; *Das elisabethanische Zeitalter;* pp. 110
[26] Rex, Richard; *Die Tudors. Englands Aufbruch in die Neuzeit 1485-1603.*; pp. 175

One of her first legal acts was instead the dismissal of all trials of heresy throughout the country, before she and her cabinet forged what is today known as the *Elizabethan Settlement*.[27]
This treaty is commonly understood to be the final compromise between the old Catholic traditions and Elisabeth's own Protestant belief. The *Alteration of Religion*[28] enforced by her father was reinstated, as well as the *Acts of Uniformity and Supremacy*. However, there were concessions made to the Catholic population, such as the tradition of sacrament, celibacy or chorals. Cramner's first *Book of Common Prayer* became the official dogma, but in return the queen disclaimed the title of *Supreme Head of Church* in favour of the more diplomatic *Supreme Governor*. All these decisions were constantly discussed during the first season of parliament in 1559, marking a new beginning of democratic political processes.

Elisabeth's second legal act was the ending of the war with Scotland and France to stop the vast inflation in England. The Convention of Edinburgh in 1560, devised by secretary of state William Cecil, was largely satisfactory for the English crown. It succeeded in establishing a cordial government in Scotland, even if the 'Auld Alliance' with France could not be broken up completely. The relations with Scotland became even more important in 1561, when the young queen Mary Stuart returned to her native country after her husband – King Francis I of France – had died. The re-established reign of a Catholic monarch on the English border became a topic of constant concern for the English government and lead to heated discussions about the marriage of Queen Elisabeth. It was widely agreed that the queen should marry as soon as possible to provide an heir to the throne – Mary Stuart had proclaimed herself to be the rightful queen of England already in 1558, because she was the granddaughter of King Henry VIII older sister Margaret. Marrying one of her lords, however, seemed difficult; it was feared that this would lead to new outbreaks of hostility among the nobles. A foreign prince was the alternative but, as the Spanish Marriage had shown, held the danger of rejection among the population. Elisabeth held cordial ties with many royal houses on the continent by lengthy considerations of their proposals, never quite agreeing to anyone.

---

[27] Esser, Raingard; *Die Tudors und die Stuarts*; pp. 73
[28] Rex, Richard; *Die Tudors. Englands Aufbruch in die Neuzeit 1485-1603.*; pp. 179

During those years the myth of the 'Virgin Queen' began, skilfully put in place to emphasize the queen's affection for her people. In the perceived 'relationship' between people and sovereign, the fact that the Queen had no family of her own, and could claim to embrace all her subjects as her children instead, played a major part.[29]

It is uncertain if Elisabeth really refused to marry from the beginning of her reign. Surely her mother's fate and her sister's desperate affection for a stranger had been the worst examples. The relations to the Spanish crown had never recovered from the tumult caused by the Spanish Marriage. Phillip himself had proposed to marry Elisabeth after his wife had died but her political intuition was to well developed even to consider this. While Elisabeth worked for a stabilisation of the Protestant belief in England – Cramner's *39 Articles* became the official dogma in 1563 – it seemed that a Catholic alliance was forming against her. The relations with Spain were tested to breaking point when English troops supported the Dutch rebellions in 1566 and English ships were charging the Spanish trade monopoly concerning the 'New World Trade'. In this political climate the message that Mary Stuart had fled from Scotland and was now seeking English sanctuary reached the queen and caused a turmoil that kept both council and parliament constantly busy for the next 20 years. Opinions varied as to what was the bigger threat to the realm:

Reclaiming the Scottish throne for Mary Stuart seemed a highly risky vernture and politically absurd. Shipping her on to the continent would enable her to return with a French or Spanish army to claim not only the Scottish, but also the English throne. Keeping her in England made her the automatical center of all catholic plots against Elisabeth's reign.[30]

Mary Stuart had not succeeded in establishing a trustworthy cabinet after her arrival in Edinburgh. All her privy counsellors were Protestant and her insistence to celebrate her own Catholic services caused civil commotions in the streets. However, she was not politically skilled enough to ensure a kind of compromise like her cousin in England. The idea of parliamentary monarchy was inaccessible for her, probably because she had left her native country at the age of five and had been educated in France at the most

---

[29] Suerbaum, Ulrich; *Das elisabethanische Zeitalter;* pp. 180
[30] Suerbaum, Ulrich; *Das elisabethanische Zeitalter;* pp. 164-65

absolutistic court of the age. The worst decision of her political career, however, was the rushed marriage with the English aristocrat Henry Lord Darnley, which caused not only a serious breach in her cordial relation with Elisabeth – who understood this move as base treachery against all agreements concerning the English succession – but also presented her with a politically useless and mentally unstable husband.

Within a few months their marriage failed and Mary found a new confidant in her Italian secretary David Riccio. King Henry was outraged and killed Riccio in his wife's rooms, almost causing her to lose the child she was carrying. Nevertheless, James Stuart – James VI of Scotland and I of England later on – was born in 1566. It was often said that he was not the son of the mentally unstable Darnley but of Riccio, who, like him, was very gifted in the fine arts.[31]

So James too was not unfamiliar with the accusation of bastardy. His mother would surely have liked to get rid of her husband, but never sought an annulment of her marriage, probably because it would have endangered James' legal status.

However, when in 1567 the house to which Mary had brought her husband to recover from a serious fever exploded and the body of King Henry was found strangled in the yard, not James', but her own position crumbled. It was widely acknowledged that she had not herself ordered the assassination, but her refusal to investigate and punish the rebels and their assumed leader James Bothwell, compromised her. Mary Stuart allowed herself to be abducted by Bothwell to Dunbar, where it was believed he raped her and forced her to marry him. Bothwell was thus the villain of this story, but a French-minded, catholic queen, who – apparently – did so little to evade the accusations of murder and adultery, still prooved too controversial for her subjects.[32]

Mary's half-brother, the Earl of Murray, lead the rebellion against her and her new husband and Mary was defeated and forced to flee to England, where she expected the help of her cousin Elisabeth.

The English government compromised on imprisoning her, hoping that her native country was to take her into custody and both sides engaged in a kind of stonewalling tactic, for no one wanted to have the accused and abdicated queen on their hands.

---

[31] Suerbaum, Ulrich; *Das elisabethanische Zeitalter*; pp. 162
[32] Maurer, Michael; *Eine kleine Geschichte Englands*; pp. 135

Mary Stuart and the English Catholics

Mary's few years on the throne were marked by a lack of judgement and skill on her part, which lost her not only the Scottish, but also the English crown.[33]

Although she had shown little political skill or ruling ability, the 'crystallisation' of rebellion around Mary Stuart began almost immediately. In Scotland her son had been made king and his council was headed by Lord Murray, who also provided the English government with the famous *Casket Letters*.[34] The authenticity of these documents could never be proven, but if Mary had written them, she was guilty of plotting to murder her husband. The casket-plot in Shakespeare's *Merchant of Venice* seems almost ironical compared to this incident.
Nevertheless, in 1569 the Duke of Norfolk was imprisoned in the Tower for his attempt to free Mary and seize power. Other lords like Suffolk and Elisabeth's all-time favourite Leicester were accused too, but escaped imprisonment by confessing. These insurgencies were not targeted at Elisabeth herself, but at her secretary Sir Cecil, because he was believed to be the leading head behind the ongoing bureaucratisation of the English government. Elisabeth was always focused on selecting her counsellors for their ability, not their nobility, which of course disgruntled many of her lords. Elisabeth also never had the wish to wipe out opposition as rigorously as her father had always done, but when the duke of Norfolk was released from the Tower and only one year later compromised again by the *Ridolfi Plot*[35], he was finally executed. The political climate had changed considerably since the imprisonment of Mary Stuart, and in 1570 Elisabeth had been officially excommunicated by the pope. Norfolk's continuous plots to marry the abdicated Mary Stuart and to set her on the English throne with the assistance of Spain and the Vatican, lead to a tightened control of Catholics throughout the country. They were now under the general suspicion of treason.

---

[33]Rex, Richard; *Die Tudors. Englands Aufbruch in die Neuzeit 1485-1603.*; pp. 202 [translation my own]
[34]Suerbaum, Ulrich; *Das elisabethanische Zeitalter;* pp. 165
[35] Esser, Raingard; *Die Tudors und die Stuarts*; pp. 79

The plots against Elisabeth's reign continued throughout the 1580ies, always helped along by Spain or France or the Vatican. In 1584 the assassination of William of Orange in the Netherlands caused the formation of the *Bond of Association*[36], a defence league sworn to protect the person of Elisabeth against 'papist' assassins. In addition, the parliament passed a law that effectively prohibited the succession of anyone involved in a plot to murder the former monarch. This measure was clearly taken against Mary Stuart, who was still alive although Elisabeth's counsellors beseeched her to execute her for murdering her husband – Elisabeth however refused, insisting that she would only put Mary to death if she would be presented with unquestionable proof that Mary was a traitor. Francis Walsingham in consequence became the head of the first 'Secret Service' in England to search for evidence that Mary Stuart was actively involved in a plot to murder Elisabeth. Such evidence was finally found in the *Babington Plot*[37] 1586, named after a Catholic nobleman who had offered Mary to find some 'gentlemen' to kill Elisabeth and to free her. Mary's written assent to this arrangement – although she and her supporters claimed it was fabricated by Walsinham – finally caused her to be put to trial. Fabricated evidence or not, even the most hesitant of Elisabeth's council members were now convinced that there was no security for the queen as long as Mary Stuart was alive and plotting to escape.[38]

Although she was convinced of Mary's guilt, Elisabeth refused for a long time to have her executed – fearing that this would serve as an example to doubt the inviolability of a ruler. In the same year England and Scotland were first 'united' by the Treaty of Berwick – a defensive alliance against invasion from Spain or France and also a notice of intent for the protection of Protestantism. Finally in 1587 Mary Stuart was convicted and beheaded with a sentence of death signed by Elisabeth, but still against her wish. Her council lost no time in executing the death sentence, even though normally it would have been the queens prerogative to decide te date and time for it. They feared – with good reason – that Elisabeth had every intention

---

[36] Suerbaum, Ulrich; *Das elisabethanische Zeitalter;* pp. 170
[37] Suerbaum, Ulrich; *Das elisabethanische Zeitalter;* pp. 171
[38] Suerbaum, Ulrich; *Das elisabethanische Zeitalter;* pp. 167

to prevaricate again and hope against hope for the natural (or unnatural) death of the troublesome Queen of Scots.[39] Elisabeth's private secretary Davison was imprisoned in the Tower for this arbitrary decision and even William Cecil spent some time in disgrace. For Phillip II of Spain, this was the last argument he needed for his invasion of England, although he had started to build his famous armada as early as 1585. The story of the Spanish Armada has an almost mythological standing in English history, but as none of the plays discussed later on shows any connection to this line of events, it will be left out in this paper. The most notable development for Elisabeth was a huge wave of loyalty and popularity rising from this immanent threat. Her *Tilbury Speech* is considered one of her most brilliant strokes of political imagery:

> [...] *My loving people, we have been persuaded by some that are careful of our safety, to take heed how we commit ourselves to armed multitudes, for fear of treachery. But I assure you, I do not desire to live in distrust of my faithful and loving people. Let tyrants fear! I have always so behaved myself that, under God, I have placed my chiefest strength and safeguard in the loyal hearts and good will of my subjects. [...] I know I have the body of a weak and feeble woman, but I have the heart and stomach of a king, and a king of England too; [...]*[40]

This speech, worthy of Shakespeare, enhanced the myth of 'Gloriana' almost as much as the actual defeat of the armada, which was caused not only by the English troops bravery but also by a lucky coincidence of the weather. But even this coincidence Elisabeth turned to her advantage. The medal pressed to celebrate the defeat bore the legend *Flavit et dissipati sunt*[41] - claiming that God himself had risen to the aid of the English queen and country. The war with Spain continued with minor operations on both sides, one of them, the raid of Cadiz, giving rise to Elisabeth's new favourite, the Earl of Essex. It is widely assumed that the Earl made the grave mistake of trying to exploit his victory in Cadiz – which was actually a failed attempt to support the Portuguese pretender against Spain that led to severe financial losses and caused Drake to fall into

---

[39] Rex, Richard; *Die Tudors. Englands Aufbruch in die Neuzeit 1485-1603.*; pp. 219
[40] Suerbaum, Ulrich; *Das elisabethanische Zeitalter;* pp. 223
[41] Suerbaum, Ulrich; *Das elisabethanische Zeitalter;* pp. 221

disgrace – in the same way Elisabeth used the armada for her popularity. This not only upset the balance of powers at court, but also severly angered the 'Cecil-Party'. More importantly however, the duke's notoriety and campaigning disturbed his queen, who would not have another star at court beside herself.[42]

Essex's power and popularity among the people of London was a problem for Elisabeth, as were his frequent offences against her authority. It is even recorded that he almost drew his sword against his queen.[43] His final downfall was initiated when he was sent to sort out the rebellion in Ireland, but instead of confronting the leader Tyrone, he was seen negotiating with him against his direct orders. All in all, his campaign ended in total disarray – half of his troops had already deserted him or died of illness, he had knighted so many of his followers that Elisabeth's counsellors already spoke of treachery and his desperate flight to England only ended when he stormed into the queen's bedroom with a sword in his hand.[44] In King Henry's days he would certainly not have lived to see the day, but Elisabeth forgave him for the time being and he was taken into custody at his own manor.

The last years of Elisabeth's reign saw many struggles with gentry and parliament, the Puritans becoming a considerably political force. The gentry's monopolies in trade were a common difficulty for the rising merchant class, and the expenses to pay for the war with Spain seriously burdened the state finances. In addition, in 1601 Elisabeth was forced after all to charge Essex with high treason. Frustrated by his loss of power and still believing in his common popularity he undertook an ominously desperate attempt on rebellion. With 200 supporters he marched from Essex House through the city of London and hoped to recruit supporters among the population – it is hoewever unclear if he really thought he could be successful in this venture.[45]

Essex's execution marked the end of the court romance that always had been an essential part of the myth of the 'virgin queen'. Elisabeth's last parliament, however, still saw her *Golden Speech*[46]

---
[42] Esser, Raingard; *Die Tudors und die Stuarts*; pp. 102
[43] Esser, Raingard; *Die Tudors und die Stuarts*; pp. 102
[44] Suerbaum, Ulrich; *Das elisabethanische Zeitalter;* pp. 240
[45] Rex, Richard; *Die Tudors. Englands Aufbruch in die Neuzeit 1485-1603.*; pp. 225
[46] Suerbaum, Ulrich; *Das elisabethanische Zeitalter;* pp. 244

as an example how personal grief never hinders the monarch in his duty – the counterexample to Macbeth.

> *I do assure you there is no prince that loves his subjects better, or whose love can countervail our love. There is no jewel, be it of never so rich a price, which I set before this jewel: I mean your love. [...] And, though God has raised me high, yet this I count the glory of my crown, that I have reigned with your loves. This makes me that I do not so much rejoice that God hath made me to be a Queen, as to be a Queen over so thankful a people.*[47]

When Queen Elisabeth died in 1603, she had given one last service to her people in turning a blind eye on the correspondences between her secretary Robert Cecil and other members of her court with her rightful heir James VI of Scotland, thus assuring his succession almost without delay.

---

[47] Suerbaum, Ulrich; *Das elisabethanische Zeitalter;* pp. 245

The Elizabethan Age

> *Slowly and mostly unnoticed a national image and perception of national unity is developing in England under Elisabeth's rule, a sense of national identity and the relationship between souvereign and subjects much closer than in other realms..*[48]

Elisabeth and her father both reigned for several decades, Elisabeth for almost 50 years, which naturally concealed the fact that the Tudor dynasty itself only covered two generations from Henry VII to his granddaughter. Nevertheless, what is known today as the 'Elizabethan Age' marks an incision in English history, a turning point for many social and political innovations. This chapter shall therefore summarize some of the aspects that will be needed for the historical analysis of Shakespeare later on, focussing on changes in society, government and religion.

Society and Trade
When King Henry VIII died, he left England with a new self-confidence after the breach with Rome, the first English bible, a new upswing of humanistic ideals and interest in classical texts, ancient mythology and historical research. The English universities provided innovations in art and science, and *The History of the World* by Sir Walter Raleigh[49] became a 'bestseller' among the gentry. This was the basis for a refinement and further development of the English language – the key condition for the composition of Shakespeare's works.
But Henry had also left behind the most peculiar class system in Europe, consisting of gentry, citizens, yeomen (estate owning farmers), trades people (craftsmen, merchants, fellows) and farmers still living in feudal bonds. The clergy, being one of the ruling classes in continental monarchies, was excluded almost completely from the balance of power in England. Henry VIII had ordered the monasteries and nunneries to be closed down, believing them to be

---

[48] Suerbaum, Ulrich; *Das elisabethanische Zeitalter;* pp. 528 [translation my own]
[49] Kenyon, J. P. 1958. *The Stuarts. A Study in English Kingship.* London & Glasgow: Collins Clear-Type Press.; pp. 26

centres of potential opposition and wanting the land and incomes of the church estates for the crown. It is therefore most interesting that Shakespeare chose a friar as disguise for his duke in *Measure for Measure*, a social class that had long been absent from the social imagery of England.

In addition to its unusual structure, the class system of Elizabethan England was more permeable than that of continental societies, allowing lawyers and merchants to climb to the highest levels of power, whilst many families of the lower gentry descended to become tradesmen. The most famous example for the opportunities of a well educated man can be found in Henry's first Lord Chancellor Wolsey, who came from a common family and had started his career as a lawyer in London. Education, knowledge and diligence became central themes in Elizabethan England, deriving from the glorification of hard work in the Protestant communities. Individual promotion and betterment were proclaimed to be signs of god's benevolence for the self-reliant believer. These strands of belief were most prominent in the Puritans and had a great effect on the American society as well. Because of the closure of the monasteries and the loss of their charitable duties, England was also one of the first countries to establish a law concerning poor and homeless people, even if this law was greatly affected by the belief that poverty equalled idleness and was a kind of godly punishment. Yet self-reliance was not enough in times of war and plagues. These difficult circumstances lead to the formation of the first merchant co-operations in England and in consequence to a greater influence of merchant interests on the parliament. *Depression conditions forced the merchants into tighter rings; government interference led them to take the parliament more seriously [...]* [50]

The loss of Calais under Mary I and the invention of the sea-compass had led to a new interest in sea trade and joint-stock companies developed, like the 'East-India' or 'Muscovy' company. The queen herself set great store by her captains, sometimes called her *sea-dogs*[51], like Hawkins or Drake, who engaged in privateer tactics during the war with Spain to provide the crown with money and weaken the enemy. Yet the sea-trade was highly risky. The 'merchant adventurers' were known to be returning from their

---

[50] Kenyon, J. P. 1958. *The Stuarts. A Study in English Kingship.*; pp. 16
[51] Suerbaum, Ulrich; *Das elisabethanische Zeitalter;* pp. 213

journeys with treasures and trading goods that made all their financiers rich – like Drake did when he returned from his circumnavigation of the world in 1580 and provided his sponsors with a gain of legendary 4000%.[52] But not all ships returned savely. Antonio's fate in *The Merchant of Venice* illustrates this prosperous but risky side of sea-trade.

In consequence of the opportunities and dangers provided by this new trade, Elisabeth's 'finance expert' John Gresham encouraged the construction of the first *Royal Exchange*[53] in London, a multi-storey building that housed stores, stocks and a meeting place for trades people and sponsors. Gresham was a friend of Sir Cecil's, who patronized him to his advantage throughout Elisabeth's reign. *They shared the conviction that sound finance was the foundation of successful government [...]*[54] How much of these developments and convictions were anticipated by Shakespeare can perhaps be guessed from the analysis of *The Merchant of Venice* or *Measure for Measure*.

Government and Monarch
It has been said before that the democratic concept of the 'king in parliament' was strengthened especially by Elisabeth. This was perhaps due to the fact that she was more willing to face opposition than her father had been, or that in her long reign more serious problems arose – there had been, for example, no decade-long discussions about Henry's marriages. However, it must be stated clearly that in the Elizabethan mentality and government the concept of separation of powers was not yet developed. Elisabeth had few counsellors that were as exclusively bound to one subject of expertise, as was John Gresham, and in addition the powers of state and church were combined in the person of the monarch.

Neither king nor parliament was concerned with such abstract concepts as sovereignty [...] What concerned them was the actual operation of government [...] monarchy, parliament, common law, prerogative and so on.[55]

---

[52] Suerbaum, Ulrich; *Das elisabethanische Zeitalter;* pp. 209
[53] Suerbaum, Ulrich; *Das elisabethanische Zeitalter;* pp. 325
[54] Williamson, James A. 1953. *The Tudor Golden Age.* London: Longmans Green.; pp. 259
[55] Kenyon, J. P.. ; *The Stuarts. A Study in English Kingship.*; pp. 25

The basis of monarchy since King Henry VII was a concept of *one body politic*[56], the full reign of the monarch in all fields of policy without hindrance or compromise. Experience, however, showed that this concept was often mutilated – for example under the reigns of Edward or Mary, who both never reigned only controlled by their own will and ability. Under Elisabeth, however, began what could be called the formation of a modern government system. She tried to find experts for different fields of policy to work closely with her privy counsellors, successfully impeded corruption and misuse of public funds and had a working alliance with her parliament, although she never granted them what would be today called the right to free speech. Many lords of noble blood and old families were exasperated to find themselves singled out from the circle of power because Elisabeth felt they were better courtiers and gentlemen than politicians and diplomats. Still, the character and individual values of her privy counsellors were of great importance – Sir Cecil for example moved through several posts, like Lord Secretary or Lord Treasurer, without loosing his standing as her most trusted advisor, even after the death of Mary Stuart. Sir Cecil, on the other hand, also was the only important lord at Elisabeth's court that was not engaged in a more or less serious celebration of the almost mystic cult of the 'virgin queen'. The distant worship of an inaccessible woman was initiated by the sonnets of Petrarcha and taken over by most courtiers. The image of a perfect gentleman in Elizabethan times was not complete without his writing at least a little poetry. Elisabeth herself was directly or indirectly the topic of many sonnets, books, plays or poems, in various 'disguises': Diana, Artemis, Astrea, Gloriana, Cynthia, Belphoebe, Bellona or Flora.[57] Edmund Spencer's *The Faerie Queen* and consequently Shakespeare's Titania are only two examples of this 'cult'.

Love was the language most commonly spoken at court.[58] The queen had nicknames for her most intimate friends and counsellors, perhaps a device to gloss over her unorthodox dominance over 'her' men. Her favourites – like Raleigh or Leicester – in consequence often kept their marriages secret, as not to be singled out from her inner

---

[56] Williamson, James A.; *The Tudor Golden Age.*; pp. 119
[57] Suerbaum, Ulrich; *Das elisabethanische Zeitalter;* pp. 198
[58] Rex, Richard; *Die Tudors. Englands Aufbruch in die Neuzeit 1485-1603.*; pp. 195

circle of her admirers. Perhaps the attitude of Portia to her suitors or the behaviour of Isabella to Angelo could be analysed in this context.

Religion and Opposition
The third important development of the Elizabethan Age, in the context of this essay, is the changes of religion. Until the Elizabethan Settlement it can be assumed that nothing like a 'common religion' existed in England. Mary's re-establishment of Catholicism had not met much opposition at first and many Catholic traditions survived under Elisabeth.
For the practical politician of 1558, the politique who viewed religion objectively, it was a choice between insular Catholicism and Protestantism, with maximum blurring of the dividing line between them.[59]
Religious non-conformism was tolerated in the time after the settlement, so long as it was not shown in any politically relevant way. The private belief was clearly subordinated to the practical administration of church and country. This tallied with Elisabeth's belief in religious tolerance, but in the days after the imprisonment of Mary Stuart, the indulgence to Catholics in England decreased. With the undermining influence of the pope's excommunication, which in fact proclaimed that every Catholic English citizen was freed from his loyalty to Elisabeth and had the right – if not the duty – to remove her from power, Catholic circles and private services were observed and persecuted by Walsingham's agents. Still, the remains of the Catholic tradition in the Anglican Church were not removed, the observations of Catholics being motivated by political necessity, not by religious doubts. With the early death of king Edward the English Reformation lost it's fanatical protestant edge.[60]
This was considered unsatisfactory by the more conservative Protestant circles and gave rise to the formation of Puritanism. The first Puritan formations in parliament were a reaction to the crisis evolving from the Ridolfi plot, the struggle over Mary Stuart's execution and the war with Spain. At court, however, the strict dogma and rigid beliefs of the Puritan circles were met with the same mild disapproval as were the conservative crypto-Catholics in the 1560ies. *The queen herself took no pleasure in belligerent*

---
[59] Williamson, James A.; *The Tudor Golden Age.*; pp. 250
[60] Maurer, Michael; *Eine kleine Geschichte Englands*; pp. 131

Puritanism [...] [61] Nevertheless, the 'Puritan movement' became a more and more considerable force in everyday England in the time following Elisabeth's reign, when the fear of a return to 'papist' traditions was enhanced. As an opposition to the Stuart reign, the Puritans not only attracted common people but gained the support of gentry and courtiers, who were disgruntled by James' continuing favours for his Scottish followers.

The hard truth is that Puritanism would never have advanced an inch without the support of the gentry, particularly in parliament [...] [62]

In the years of King James' reign, the great Puritan migration began towards the settlements of New England and Virginia and united Puritans, Dissenters and other conservative Protestant groups, but also political hardliners and discontent noblemen. For Shakespeare the Puritans were most important in their continued feud against the theatres of London, for they were supposed to cause loose manners and idleness among the citizens. A closer look at their connection to the Elizabethan and Jacobean drama shall be given later on.

---

[61] Williamson, James A.; *The Tudor Golden Age.;* pp. 317
[62] Kenyon, J. P.; *The Stuarts. A Study in English Kingship.*; pp. 21

James I and the Union of the Crowns

James entry into England was hailed by jubilant crowds, but his popularity among his southern subjects and the political circles of the court decreased quickly.[63]

Although kingship had passed to James VI of Scotland when he was only a baby, by the time he arrived in England to finally unite the two crowns, he was already in his late thirties. He had been well educated by humanist and Protestant teachers and was known to be more of an intellectual than a practical politician. He had published books concerning questions of law, theology and occultism i.e. *Daemonology* (1597), *The True Law of Free Monarchies* (1598) or *The Basilikon Doron* (1599).[64] He was also known to be a patron of the fine arts and had theatre plays and masques performed regularly at his court. This brought him in close contact to Shakespeare's plays, even if Shakespeare himself was not regularly received at court.

James had suffered much turbulence in his youth, struggles among the lords and his Lord Protector and finally the exile of his intimate friend and cousin Lennox. He had married the Protestant Anne of Denmark and made his famous ship journey to Norway to lead his queen home, when she was hindered by storms. He had also faced a strong Presbyterian opposition during his reign in Scotland. The conservative Presbyterian circles had called for a submission of the crown under the power of 'god's representatives' on earth – a claim that James had refused wholeheartedly and answered with anti-Presbyterian decrees. Handing over even a small part of his power was unacceptable; because for all his Protestant belief and humanist education he cherished the strong conviction of the divine right of kings. Thus, he himself believed to be 'god's chosen representative'. When he was crowned as king of England in 1603 it can be assumed that all this was well known to Elisabeth's courtiers and counsellors, who had, despite her ban, been corresponding with him for a while before she died, smoothing his way to the throne. Nevertheless, the king's temperament, which was said to be varying from melancholic

---

[63] Esser, Raingard; *Die Tudors und die Stuarts*; pp. 110 [translation my own]
[64] Maurer, Michael; *Eine kleine Geschichte Englands*; pp. 170

moods to rough joviality, surprised the courtiers. The king's bawdy humour and his winking blasphemy caused uncertainty and indignation among Elisabeth's ageing lords.[65]

After the coronation James tried to form his own privy council consisting of his long-term advisors he had brought from Scotland and Elisabeth's skilled counsellors. Yet the positions became entrenched very soon, the Scottish lords unwilling to lose their trusted positions, the English lords set on stressing that England's needs should have priority in this union of crowns.[66] The people of London meanwhile soon realized that habits had changed under the new regime. Queen Elisabeth had always set great store by her popularity and often sought the contact with the people of London or her parliamentarians. Her summer passages through the country had often included folk banquets and she had encouraged parades and games in London. King James was more concerned for his privacy and divided his time strictly between his public and private personas.[67]

In 1604, James I was officially proclaimed king of 'Great Britain' by his first parliament and the first attempt at a Union Jack was made the official flag. The same year also saw the well-known *Hampton Court Conference*[68], during which the king made his famous defence of the continuity of the bishop-church system: *No bishop, No king.*[69] Presbyterian movements aiming at the destruction of the 'papist' structures of clerical power were discouraged in England as they had been in Scotland. In addition, the conference ended with the king's order to compile a new official bible for the whole population of Britain. The authorized *King James Bible* was consequently published in 1611.[70] His upholding of the clerical traditions and his success in signing a truce with Spain in the Treaty of London lead to a short-lived upswing in his popularity, due to his image as *rex pacificus*[71]. But the opposition to the Stuart reign was forming and

---

[65] Kenyon, J. P.; *The Stuarts. A Study in English Kingship.*; pp. 33
[66] Maurer, Michael; *Eine kleine Geschichte Englands*; pp. 173
[67] Maurer, Michael; *Eine kleine Geschichte Englands*; pp. 167
[68] Esser, Raingard; *Die Tudors und die Stuarts*; pp. 123
[69] Esser, Raingard; *Die Tudors und die Stuarts*; P 123
[70] Kenyon, J. P.; *The Stuarts. A Study in English Kingship.*; pp. 38
[71] Esser, Raingard; *Die Tudors und die Stuarts*; pp. 127

had its first appearance in the noted *Gunpowder Plot* of 1605[72] - a curious alliance of crypto-Catholic and anti-absolutistic elements set on destroying both king and parliament in one go. The 5th of November was afterwards christened 'Guy Fawkes Day' – after the assumed leader of the rebels – to be a lasting example for the immanent Catholic threat to king and country. The fear of 'papist' plots and a revival of the Catholic traditions had outlived both Mary Stuart and Elisabeth and were to turn on the Stuart regime in the outbreak of the civil-war.

There are several theories why King James' popularity dwindled so quickly after his coronation, or why he was not able to provide a solution to the pressing social problems of his time. This parliament presented him with the owing problems that had been handed down to him from Elisabeth's reign – the fight for free speech, the desolate state finance or the hated trade monopolies. The king, it was felt, should live of his own properties and only in times of need and war should a parliament be convened – this view was however already anachronistical in the 16th century.[73]

The king's lack of austerity in times of crisis – especially compared to the clever economy of Elisabeth – caused resentments among the population. Soon the courts of the crown princes Henry and, after him, Charles were set as ascetic and military focussed counterexamples to the king's masques and feasts. But the members of parliament were even more worried about James' theories of monarchy. In the time of his reign he took to giving long speeches in front of the parliament concerning his theories of divine right and the infallibility of a ruler – absolutistic ideals in short. This caused a stir of fear among the members of parliament, who saw the rights and freedom of England endangered.

Yet the king was even less able to conciliate the struggling lords at his court than he was reassuring the parliament. Queen Elisabeth had always sought to play out one party against the other and thus reigning unimpeded. James' patronizing however was entirely focussed on personal sympathy rather than political use or the individual ability of the patronized. *The king's extravagance involved him in a host of difficulties.*[74] The delicate balance of

---

[72] Maurer, Michael; *Eine kleine Geschichte Englands*; pp. 172
[73] Maurer, Michael; *Eine kleine Geschichte Englands*; pp. 172-73
[74] Kenyon, J. P. ; *The Stuarts. A Study in English Kingship.* ; pp. 39

political interest and powers kept intact by Elisabeth slowly crumbled as the political expertise of the king's chosen counsellors decreased, while the grudge of the English gentry against their Scottish counterparts rose during the years.

The Dawn of Revolution

> *The relationship of this new kinf to his English subjects was from the first overshadowed by the mistrust and even hatred that the English bore towards all Scotsmen.* [75]

Shakespeare retired to Stratford in 1611 and so did not witness the beginning of the Stuart's downfall in King James' last years directly. Yet the question remains how much of the pre-civil-war mentality was foreshadowed in *Macbeth* or even *The Winter's Tale*. A few last aspects of the reign of King James shall therefore be given to round off this first part of historical elaboration.

In 1610 King James caused uproar in London when he closed down the parliament after it had unapologetically refused to bestow him with taxes to finance his court. The state finance was still in a most desolate state, the debts made by Elisabeth to pay for the war with Spain had yet not been repaid. In addition the court could not pay its running expenses from the king's leasing receipts alone, even Elisabeth had not been able to manage that any longer in her final years, in defiance of all her financial skill and canniness. But the king's ill repute for being wasteful and extravagant, granting huge gifts to his queen and favourites, counted against him, as it had not done against Elisabeth. The parliament refused resolutely to finance this life-style and criticised harshly James' obsession for hunting, his all but official bisexuality and reports from noblemen about vast carousals and excessive feasts at court. All these excesses were taken as evidence that the king was not inclined to rehabilitate the state finances, even if more taxes would be granted to him.[76] James himself could not tolerate being criticised by his subjects and consequently dismissed the parliament immediately. This however did not solve his financial problems. In 1611 he therefore created the purchasable noble title of baronet, as a new source of income for the crown and he carried on giving trade monopolies to his most favoured courtiers. These favours had been a source of exasperation for so long among the tradesmen of London and it is astounding that

---

[75] Maurer, Michael; *Eine kleine Geschichte Englands*; pp. 173 [translation my own]
[76] Kenyon, J. P.; *The Stuarts. A Study in English Kingship.*; pp. 41

James should have missed the explosive power of that political decision.

In 1613 then began what could be called the Stuart's return to Catholicism. The king had since the Treaty of London desired to insure the peace with his Catholic neighbours. Now he devised a plan for a second 'Spanish Marriage' concerning his son, the crown prince Charles and the Infanta Maria Anna, the granddaughter of Phillip II.

The whole impact of the 'papist fear', the old stories about Bloody Mary and the terror of Spanish dominance reappeared among the population and a solid opposition formed to prevent this replay of history. In the same year however the court and people of London saw the beginnings of a tremendous scandal in the king's inner circle, which is of some interest for this essay, because of the accusations of witchcraft and daemonic powers involved.

In 1613 King James rehabilitated the Duke of Norfolk and his family the Howard clan, which had been in disgrace ever since the Ridolfi plot.

The Howards sought an alliance with the king's favourite Robert Carr and had the marriage of the Countess of Essex annulled because of impotence, so that she could marry her lover Carr. King James supported this marriage and made Robert the new Earl of Somerset. Perhaps the title of Somerset stood under a bad star since the reign of King Edward, for three years later Somerset fell when his wife was accused of having poisoned a man called Overbury.

He was said to have discovered her black magic circle and wanted to have her persecuted for performing witchcraft and daemonic services at the king's court.[77] These accusations not only compromised Somerset and the Norfolk clan, but also demolished King James' popularity even more. He sought to repair the damage by dismissing Carr and turned to a new advisor – George Villiers, who would become Duke of Buckingham before long. James' knowledge of human nature seems to have been unfortunately limited and Buckingham played a major role in the outbreak of the civil-war, concentrating on him the people's and the noblemen's fury alike.

But as Shakespeare died in the same year the Countess of Essex was accused of witchcraft, the relevance of King James' reign for this essay does not extent to the downfall of his son.

---

[77] Kenyon, J. P.; *The Stuarts. A Study in English Kingship.*; pp. 49

It can only be assumed anyway if Shakespeare himself foresaw some of these troublesome events in his later works and nothing can be said of his political ambition one he had left the stage and London. The political impact of his theatre however and the Elizabethan and Jacobean theatre in general shall be analysed in the next chapter.

Elisabeth, James and English Renaissance Theatre

> *The court [...] was itself a theatre of sorts, in that it habitants lived by social and political role-playing and game-playing, and thus was particularly suited to examination by the theatre proper.*[78]

The 'invention' of commercial theatre during the Elizabethan Age has been researched and documented by countless critics and historians in the last centuries. The history and development of the theatre business however is of only marginal importance for this essay and this chapter will therefore focus especially on the *interconnectedness*[79] of theatre and authority, stage and court. To provide a conclusive picture of Shakespeare's political allusions in the literary analysis following in the next part of the essay, it feels necessary to analyse what can be known of the relation between monarchy and theatre during the English renaissance. This first part will therefore focus on what we know of Elisabeth's and James' views towards this art-form and its propagandistic uses. Then the focus will shift to what we can know of Shakespeare's biography and a general overview of the historical and political impact of his work. When the first theatre opened in London in 1567 it gave rise to a whole new range of professions, of which the players or actors easily were the most popular. *The speed with which the acting-profession gained respect probably derived from the commercial theatre's rapid and widespread popularity [...]*[80]

Theatre and games provided the first entertainment business in Europe during the renaissance and London in particular held more

---

[78] Lancashire, Anne. 1991. "Recent Studies in Elizabethan and Jacobean Drama." In: Patten, Robert L.(ed.). *Studies in English Literature 1500-1900*. Houston, Texas: Johns Hopkins University Press, Vol. 31. pp. 385-421.; pp. 400

[79] Lancashire, Anne. 1991. "Recent Studies in Elizabethan and Jacobean Drama."; pp. 398

[80] Goldstein, Gary B. 2004. "Did Queen Elisabeth Use the Theatre for Social and Political Propaganda?" In: The Shakespeare-Oxford Society. *The Oxfordian*. Port Washington: Kennikat Press; Vol. 7. pp. 153-169.; pp. 159

theatres than any other dwelling in Europe.[81] As the biggest city in Europe it also imported ideas, politics and commerce to other parts of the continent, the commercial theatre being an essential part of the social imagery. *The newly born commercial theatre was the only mass medium during the reign of Elisabeth I capable of addressing the broader spectrum of private and public issues [...]*[82]
Role-play and ceremony presented one of the major themes of the century, from the parades and processions of clergy and parliament to the political ceremonies of court. The commercial theatre however was not in particular concerned with education or edification, as were the ecclesiastic ceremonies or the performances of saint-lives or biblical stories during the Middle Ages. This lack of moral standing was one reason why the theatres were so bitterly fought by the Puritan movement. Another was the all but outlawed position of the theatre buildings, crowding on the edge of London, neighbouring brothels and bear-fighting arenas, or sometimes capitalizing on the closure of monasteries to buy estates inside the town – like the Blackfriars 1597 – and thereby be protected from the common law. Yet the Puritan preachers were only the most ferocious heads of the opposition forming against the theatres.[83]

The city council of London also registered their concern with Elisabeth's Privy Council about the commercial theatre. On the one hand it disturbed the holy order of the universe being divided into rulers and ruled by presenting common people in the costumes and habits of kings. On the other hand it provided a threat to the public order, as the plays openly presented examples for murder, betrayal and rebellion.[84] Yet queen and Privy Council hesitated to persecute or close the theatres, perhaps unwilling to forgo their own entertainment, but perhaps also because it presented a highly useful medium of mass manipulation.

---

[81] Suerbaum, Ulrich; *Das elisabethanische Zeitalter;* pp. 399

[82] Goldstein, Gary B.; *Did Queen Elisabeth Use the Theatre for Social and Political Propaganda?*; pp. 153

[83] *[...] the cause of plagues is sin [...] and the cause of sin are plays: therefore the cause of plagues are plays. A Sermon at St. Paul's Cross* as quoted in: Suerbaum, Ulrich; *Das elisabethanische Zeitalter;* pp. 429

[84] Goldstein, Gary B.; *Did Queen Elisabeth Use the Theatre for Social and Political Propaganda?*; pp. 434

It was purpose-build for touring and was intended to spread the queen's name and Protestant ideology into far-flung reaches of the kingdom.[85]

Elisabeth as the last representative of the Tudor reign presided over a period of change and progress, as has been elaborated before, and had to find a balance of power between old remains of the feudal system, the new rise of the merchant class and reforms of government and religion. To keep this balance and forestall unpleasant opposition she made use of the *Company of Stationers*[86] originally founded by her sister Mary I. This restricted the publishing business to manuscripts seen and licensed by queen, Privy Council or church. This policy was highly effective too, as only four cases of illegal printing ensued during Elisabeth's reign – the most spectacular the famous Martin Marplerate, a conservative Puritan, who published tractates offending queen and bishops as usurpers of divine rule, according to the Puritan belief that god, as represented in the bible, is the only ruler of mankind.[87]

Elisabeth herself was always considered to be a very able politician and highly skilled in 'acting her part'. Already her coronation served as a first public performance of her new regime and presented a carefully rehearsed show of public interest and graciousness.[88]

While it was however highly important to be seen on those public events, it was Elisabeth's great concern not to be displayed as a character on the common stage. For this reason a decree was issued, prohibiting the display of living rulers on the common stage. This measure was taken to prevent the *desacralisation*[89] of royal ceremony

---

[85] Skura, Meredith Anne. 2000. "Recent Studies in Tudor and Stuart Drama." In: Patten, Robert L.(ed.). *Studies in English Literature 1500-1900.* Houston, Texas: Johns Hopkins University Press, Vol. 40. pp. 355-389.; pp. 367

[86] Goldstein, Gary B.; *Did Queen Elisabeth Use the Theatre for Social and Political Propaganda?*; pp. 154

[87] Goldstein, Gary B.; *Did Queen Elisabeth Use the Theatre for Social and Political Propaganda?*; pp. 158

[88] *[...] she displayed her considerable skill as an actress to sustain a dazzling performance in which she won the hearts of her people.,* McCoy, Richard C. 1989. "Thou Idol Ceremony: Elisabeth I., The Henriad, and the Rites of the English Monarchy." In: Zimmerman, Susan; Weissman, Ronald F. E. (eds.). *Urban Life in the Renaissance.* Cranbury, NJ: Associated University Presses. pp. 240-68.; pp. 244

[89] McCoy, Richard C. 1989. "Thou Idol Ceremony: Elisabeth I., The Henriad, and the Rites of the English Monarchy."; pp. 250

and authority, an attempt to balance the two counterparts of being a 'peoples' person' and an inaccessible idol. In 1574 the Earl of Leicester's group of players first gained the permission to perform at court, thus widening the scope of theatre from the common to the aristocratic audience. Nevertheless, the whole performance was under the control of the Master of Revels, as were all royal pastime amusements. This control was however widened by Elisabeth to the whole city of London by 1581, providing the full control of the government not only over the publishing but now also over the performance of plays. This measure was another clever move of media control and ensured the ban on displaying the royal rites and ceremonies in unsuited circumstances. Yet these restrictions did not concern Elisabeth's enemies. Many historical sources account for complaints raised especially by Spanish ambassadors, who were openly ridiculed on London's stages, as was King Phillip himself occasionally. In the 1590ies the satire also included the Vatican and – in anxious anticipation of his succession to the throne – *the poorest prince in Christendom*[90], King James of Scotland.

Consequently to the development of media control many plays about the 'good old days' of Elisabeth's rule issued under the reign of James I, displaying the monarch with reverence but nevertheless including dialogues and gestures that would have been considered impertinent in 'real life', exposing the *void behind the illusion*.[91] Some critics claim the distorting powers of Shakespeare's works in presenting his queen, for example in *Venus and Adonis* or *The Rape of Lucrece*.[92] Shakespeare's plays present such situations when he includes Richard II speech about the invulnerability of a ruler shortly before his defeat in battle (III, 2), or when Henry V first uses the word 'idol' to describe his standing among his subjects (IV, 1).[93] The idolisation of Elisabeth however was not to last during her long reign. She may have been worshipped and unchallenged while her

---

[90] see Goldstein, Gary B.; *Did Queen Elisabeth Use the Theatre for Social and Political Propaganda?*; pp. 166

[91] McCoy, Richard C.; Thou Idol Ceremony: *Elisabeth I., The Henriad, and the Rites of the English Monarchy*.; pp. 254

[92] Marcus, Leah S. 1992. "Recent Studies in Elizabethan and Jacobean Drama." In: Patten, Robert L.(ed.). *Studies in English Literature 1500-1900*. Houston, Texas: Johns Hopkins University Press, Vol. 32. pp. 361-401.; pp. 369

[93] McCoy, Richard C.; Thou Idol Ceremony: *Elisabeth I., The Henriad, and the Rites of the English Monarchy*.; pp. 258

Gloriana image lasted, but in her last years this authority crumbled under the strain of war, inflation and misused favouritism.
The official portraits of her last years were perhaps more successful than were courtly performances [...] the figure is heavily encrusted with the mystical trappings of majesty.[94]
When King James acceded to the throne in 1603 he set out to be the bringer of peace to a united kingdom by his divine right to rule. His *Basilikon Doron – the most important statement on kingship*[95] - and his other literary achievements were evidence to his new subjects that their king was well aware of the possibilities and uses of literature. Consequently James not only continued the policy of media control established by Elisabeth, he also tried to impose some subsequent measures. Spencer's *Faerie Queen* for example was banned from publishing because of its propagandistic – and consequently compromising – display of Mary Stuart. Perhaps the king felt that digging up those 'old stories' would be bad publicity for his accession. Nevertheless, the banned *The Faerie Queen* and the later *View of the Present State of Ireland*[96] provided a precedent for the suppression of what can be considered the accurate view of 17th century realpolitik. This serves as another example for King James' strong conviction that the *mysterie of the King's power*[97] could not and should not be displayed to the common subjects. In contrast to Elisabeth, who 'only' feared to be displayed in an inadequate way, James refused to let himself be displayed or questioned at all; and – in contrast to Elisabeth again – he set out to be his own annalist. To this purpose James concentrated on describing and communicating his views on sovereignty to his council and parliament, but comparing the *Tilbury Speech* and the *True Law of the Free Monarchies,* a definite change in 'publicity policy' is discernible – *the subjects love and good affection* is replaced with *his subjects fear and* subjection.[98] One has to note however that either image was acceptable for a ruler, as long as his politic served the 'common good'. Yet James' popularity suffered in his years of power in

---

[94] McCoy, Richard C.; Thou Idol Ceremony: *Elisabeth I.*, The Henriad, *and the Rites of the English Monarchy.*; pp. 260
[95] Goldberg, Jonathan; *James I. and the Politics of Literature.*; pp. xi
[96] Goldberg, Jonathan; *James I. and the Politics of Literature.*; pp. 9
[97] Goldberg, Jonathan; *James I. and the Politics of Literature.*; pp. 56
[98] Goldberg, Jonathan; *James I. and the Politics of Literature.*; pp. 28

England from his hesitation to display himself in public, he was not what would be called a 'peoples' person' and he had no interest – or skill – in balancing the two sides of his publicity, the common and the inaccessible. It is therefore probable that the king tried to enlist other means to promote his publicity and literature and drama served just this purpose. *The Triumphs of King James*[99] were published in 1610, the year of James' first serious struggles with the parliament and masques played at court depicted him as Solomon, David, Caesar or Apollo in the fine tradition of the Elisabeth cult. At least in these secluded circles the king wholly appreciated the theatrical imagery of the 'political person', also including the difference between *outward appearance* and *inward intention*[100] Elisabeth had used to great effect.

Shakespeare and his company rose to be the king's servants only months after King James accession, a fact that has often lead to the conclusion that James had a great liking for theatre plays and Shakespeare in particular.[101] However, as will be explored in the next chapter, Shakespeare himself never showed ambitions to become a noted part of the royal household. King James' patronage in addition could not exclusively focus on the theatre, owing to the widespread network of authority and influence in the 17th century 'empire' - *[...] a body politic with a prince but composed of constitutions such as the peerage, Parliament, and the city guilds [...]* [102]

Nevertheless, the status as The King's Men can be assumed to have had its benefits even if they were not excluded form closures because of plague or the ban to perform on Sabbath days.[103] It provided for example the opportunity to travel the country while the theatres were closed down and gave Shakespeare ample opportunity to see his plays performed before a royal audience. Yet Shakespeare's plays were never exclusively written for court performances, but this does not eliminate the possibility that some of them include some allusion to the ruler of the time – although as we have seen such allusions

---

[99] Goldberg, Jonathan; *James I. and the Politics of Literature.*; pp. 56

[100] Goldberg, Jonathan; *James I. and the Politics of Literature.*; pp. 114

[101] see Goldberg, Jonathan; *James I. and the Politics of Literature.*; pp. 231

[102] Barrol, Leeds. 1991. *Politics, Plague and Shakespeare's Theatre. The Stuart Years.* Ithaca & London: Cornell University Press.; pp. 24

[103] Barrol, Leeds. 1991. *Politics, Plague and Shakespeare's Theatre. The Stuart Years;* pp. 34

would have to be very carefully placed. Nevertheless, the London stages were not hesitant in some respects to make fun of figures of authority, such as aristocrats, clergymen or the king's native country Scotland, again continuing the Elizabethan tradition. From the fact that such allusions were seldom cut out, as far as we know, from the performances at court, it can be assumed that the king tolerated such general ridicule, where he would certainly have punished personal criticism.[104] The significant upswing of court performances presents another argument for critics and historians to believe in King James' interest for the theatre. However this must not necessarily lead to the conclusion that the king had a greater linking for this art-form than his predecessor, a courtier named Dudley Garleton is even quoted *he takes no extraordinary pleasure in them.*[105] The number of plays acted before the king must be seen in another light than the whole number of court performances, which could be ordered by the queen, the crown prince, or other members of the royal family as well. The fact that there had been no royal family in England for the last 45 years of Elisabeth's rule may be an important factor in this consideration.[106] It can however not be denied that Shakespeare's company was granted several favours, for example by the Earl of Pembroke. Historical sources relay a personal friendship between the earl and Richard Burbage, another actor and shareholder of the King's Men.[107] The conclusion, however, that this association frees Shakespeare of all connections with king and court whatsoever is highly partial. The fact that Shakespeare did not have any 'personal relation' to the king or even high ranking aristocrats does not necessarily implicate his disinterest in the development of monarchy. Even the fact that the favours granted to the King's Men were perhaps the achievement of Burbage rather than Shakespeare does not exclude the probability that these connections to the inner circles of power had some effect on the plays written for the company by Shakespeare.

---

[104] see Goldberg, Jonathan; *James I. and the Politics of Literature.*; pp. 232
[105] Goldberg, Jonathan; *James I. and the Politics of Literature.*; pp. 27
[106] see Barrol, Leeds; *Politics, Plague and Shakespeare's Theatre. The Stuart Years.*; pp. 26
[107] see Barrol, Leeds; *Politics, Plague and Shakespeare's Theatre. The Stuart Years.*; pp. 41

The Author Shakespeare

It is as if there where two separate conceptual entities: the dramatist and his plays.[108]

In the last chapters of this essay the focus has steadily narrowed, from the elaboration of English renaissance history, to the relation of monarch and literature and it has now reached the person of Shakespeare himself. A short account of the life behind the plays seems unavoidable for the historical literary analysis in the next part of the paper; however, the sources for such an account are very limited. Although there are many documents and records signed by Shakespeare or mentioning him[109,] those signatures and references tell us next to nothing about the person Shakespeare, his character, opinions, believes or political position. This uncertainty may be the true reason for the endless re-interpretations of Shakespeare's works, each including the assumed point of view of the 'author behind the character', searching for evidence for *a man with power.*[110]

We know that Shakespeare was born in 1564 in the village of Stratford-upon-Avon and that his father was a tradesman and mayor of the village. But then already the guesswork ensues, beginning with a bankruptcy of the family and the exclusion of the father from all communal positions. Did the financial problems lead to this exclusion or was there a crypto-Catholic background to the family that was inconvenient for the townspeople in the political climate?[111] It is next guessed that Shakespeare underwent a good education – either in the free school of Stratford or by assumed Catholic tutors – which was essential for the belief of self-improvement in the 'new middle-class'.

---

[108] Barrol, Leeds; *Politics, Plague and Shakespeare's Theatre. The Stuart Years.*; pp. 4

[109] Suerbaum, Ulrich; *Das elisabethanische Zeitalter;* pp. 346

[110] Worden, Blair; *Shakespeare and Politics.;* In: *Shakespeare and Politics*; pp. 22-44; pp. 23

[111] see Badawi, M. M.; *Background to Shakespeare.*; London: Macmillan Press 1981; pp. 16

If he was however the model for middle-class self-reliance, as some historians suggest him to be[112], is questionable especially with regard to his supposed Catholicism. His potential later career covers a whole range of different professions – all of them displayed in his later work – such as schoolmaster, which would account for his knowledge of society, lawyer because of his frequent use of trials and judicial terms, soldier because of his display of military ranks, etc. Also medical or scholarly occupations are possible.[113] There are indeed so many possible careers to fill the missing years of Shakespeare's biography – between the birth of his second and third child in Stratford and his reappearance in London – that the *actual time for playwriting seems limited.*[114] As a playwright he was however not mentioned before 1592, when his 'fellow author' Robert Greene described him as an *upstart crow*[115] and a threat to well-educated, if not aristocratic, authors. However, it must be taken into consideration that the theatre was still a rather new phenomenon in England and that the profession of playwright or dramatist was not commonly acknowledged by the public. In addition, the production of plays was not considered to be literature in the sense of Chaucer or even Sophocles. A playwright 'produced' his texts on a day to day basis and for a very short-lived purpose. This timeliness had its drawbacks as far as undying literary fame was concerned, but it was highly useful for propaganda. *To be a player was continually to be policed.*[116]

By the time Shakespeare arrived in London dramatist and players were watched closely by the government, not only because of the steady mistrust of the city authorities.

In 1594 Shakespeare was exclusively writing for the Lord Chamberlain's Men, the Earl of Leicester's company, who would become the King's Men under James I later on. Yet he also wrote the poetical works *Venus and Adonis* and *The Rape of Lucrece* – a better respected form of literature in Elizabethan England – in times when

---

[112] see Suerbaum, Ulrich; *Das elisabethanische Zeitalter;* pp. 347
[113] see Badawi, M. M.; *Background to Shakespeare.;* pp. 19
[114] Worden, Blair; *Shakespeare and Politics.;* pp. 23
[115] *Testament of Robert Greene* as quoted in: Badawi, M. M.; *Background to Shakespeare.;* pp. 19
[116] Barrol, Leeds; *Politics, Plague and Shakespeare's Theatre. The Stuart Years.;* pp. 9

the theatres were closed due to the plague in 1593. Although Shakespeare was never a member of an aristocratic household or the receiver of a regular patronage, like for example John Donne[117], both of these epic poems are dedicated to the Earl of Southampton, which has lead to the presumption of a close friendship between author and aristocrat. This would of course contradict the theory that Shakespeare had no insights into the inner circles of the court, but there is no proof that Shakespeare and Southampton were connected in any way beside the dedication, which may hint at a kind of non-recurring patronage, which may have been only flattery.

Sometimes Shakespeare is also connected to the Earl of Pembroke, whose friendship to Richard Burbage has been mentioned earlier. The dedication of Shakespeare's sonnets to *W.H.*[118] has lead to the consideration of William Herbert, Earl of Pembroke, as the addressee, in addition to the possibility of Henry Wriothesley, Earl of Southampton. Neither connection can of course be conclusively proven.

Shakespeare's poetic endeavours, however, seemed to have been either financially unsuccessful or unattractive to him, for he returned to the common stage after the plague was over. Some critics interpret this short-lived venture into the respected realm of authorship as an attempt to secure a more reliable post, perhaps in the household of Southampton. Shakespeare's two poems won him a reputation among the connaisseurs of literature, free from the 'taint' of theatre productions.[119] The composition of poetry was at any rate a more suited occupation for a gentleman and many of Elisabeth's gentlemen, who felt their lack of creativity, paid others to write it for them.

Others assume that Shakespeare saw no point in writing dramas, when there was no theatre open to rehearse or perform them in.[120] This incident is an excellent example to demonstrate the limits of a biography only consisting of documents and publishing dates. We know when *Lucrece* was written, but to the *why* there can only be

---

[117] *Barrol, Leeds; Politics, Plague and Shakespeare's Theatre. The Stuart Years.;* pp. 10
[118] Badawi, M. M.; *Background to Shakespeare.*; pp. 20
[119] Suerbaum, Ulrich; *Das elisabethanische Zeitalter;* pp. 356
[120] Barrol, Leeds; *Politics, Plague and Shakespeare's Theatre. The Stuart Years.*; pp. 17

assumptions. It may even be probable that Shakespeare enjoyed the closure of the theatres, because it gave him time to pursue another form of literary occupation that had been lying low in the day to day struggle from performance to performance.

In 1595 Shakespeare became shareholder in the Chamberlain's Men – the most favoured company under Elisabeth – and his plays were more widely acknowledged. One year later he was even able to acquire a coat of arms for his family in Stratford. The document explicitly mentions Shakespeare as a 'player', not even as a playwright and emphasises the importance of the Shakespeare family since the reign of King Henry VII. But as this was the custom in these days whenever a coat of arms was granted, not much of Shakespeare's importance for the English crown can be deduced from it.[121] In 1599 Shakespeare then moved on to become shareholder in the Globe Theatre as well, ensuring a regular income even in times when none of his own plays were performed there. In 1601, however, the company was temporarily involved in the unfortunate Essex rebellion, having been paid to perform Shakespeare's *Richard II* the evening before the coup. However, the queen seemed to take the role of the players in this affair not very seriously – even if she uttered the famous line *I am Richard II. Know ye not that?*[122] – and they were asked to *perform again at court only a fortnight after the incident.*[123]

When King James acceded to the throne in 1603 he lost no time to issue a decree to make the Lord Chamberlain's Men The King's Men instead. The official document is dated 19th of May 1603, barely a month after the king's accession, and names *Lawrence Fletcher, William Shakespeare, Richard Burbage*[124] and others to be members of the royal household forthwith. Furthermore it claims that they are entitled to perform in the Globe Theatre, but also in every other part of the country and at court, with the specification that the company

---

[121] see Suerbaum, Ulrich; *Das elisabethanische Zeitalter;* pp. 360

[122] see i.a. Wilson, Richard. 2002. "Shakespeare in Hate. Performing the Virgin Queen." In: *Poetica. Schriften zur Literaturwissenschaft.* München: Wilhelm Fink Verlag, Vol. 34. pp. 149-167.; pp. 155

[123]. Barrol, Leeds; *Politics, Plague and Shakespeare's Theatre. The Stuart Years.*; pp. 22

[124] Mahler, Andreas. 2002. *Shakespeare's Subkulturen. Typen, Tricks, Topographien.* Passau: Stutz Verlag.; pp. 107

has the right to require any help from the local sheriffs and authorities.[125] So to a small extent the protection of the king did guarantee at least a slight betterment in the condition of the King's Men.

When Shakespeare retired to Stratford completely in 1611, he did so as a wealthy man, having earned proportions of the Globe's proceeds and the payment grated by the Master of Revels for court performances. Although he had never published his works himself, tried to sell them to his advantage or was endued with useful 'business contacts', he had acquired a fairly large estate and a mansion in the centre of the village where he lived until his death in 1616.

In his historical works Shakespeare seems to offer very contradicting images concerning the English renaissance policy – one the one hand a defender of the monarch's right to rule (*King John, Richard III*), on the other a revolutionary and rebel (*Richard II*). Which image will be presented in the plays where no ruler is displayed by name, shall be inquired in the literary analysis later on.

---

[125]see Mahler, Andreas. 2002. *Shakespeare's Subkulturen. Typen, Tricks, Topographien;* pp. 107

Shakespeare and English Monarchy

The theatrical Ego and the royal Ego are so intertwined in Shakespeare's Richard that the Actor-as-King time and again reflects the King-as-Actor.[126]

Shakespeare's works have long since been analysed in historical contexts, most notably of course the history plays. The description and refurbishment of English history was after all highly popular in the Elizabethan Age, as has been described before. Still Shakespeare's plays have seen many – and often contradictory – re-workings over the centuries, to describe their political impact: *neo-conservative, Protestant, Catholic, Republican, Liberal, Tory, Marxist, high Anglican*[127], Feminist, Communist etc. Each of these readings finds its own arguments and creates its own image of Shakespeare, and none can easily be discarded. Shakespeare's habit of combining and 're-working' all kinds of influences and narratives into his plots and characters, makes a conclusive interpretation of Shakespeare's intention even more difficult. The sources of Shakespeare's plays seem to include adaptations and references of classical sources and narratives, contemporary popular plays by other authors or timely trials and sermons. It is undeniable that Shakespeare for example used the opposition and heated sermons of the Puritans to ridicule their self-righteous manner and hypocritical pompousness in his plays – for example in the character of Malvolio in *Twelfth Night*.[128] Yet this satire should be of only marginal political importance, as it has been shown before that neither Elisabeth nor James showed a special goodwill towards the Puritan movement. But as an educated man in the Elizabethan Age Shakespeare also had access to all sorts of contemporary political

---

[126] Höfele, Andreas. 1997. "The Great Image of Authority. Königsbilder in Shakespeare's Theatre." In: Deutsche Shakespeare-Gesellschaft. *Shakespeare Jahrbuch*. Bochum: Kamp Verlag, Vol. 133. pp. 77-98.; pp. 88 [translation my own]

[127] Joughin, John J. 2004. "Shakespeare and Politics: An Introduction." In: Alexander, Catherine M. S. (ed.). *Shakespeare and Politics*. Cambridge: Cambridge Univ. Press. pp.1-22.; pp. 1

[128] see Coyle, Martin. 2001. "Shakespeare: Theatrical and Historical Contexts." In: Rylance, Rick; Simons, Judy (eds.). *Literature in Context*. Houndmills: Palgrave. pp. 15-33.; pp. 28

theories, such as the works of More, Bacon, Montaigne or Machiavelli. These new developments of realpolitik were part of the balance of power Elisabeth kept intact for a long time, but they were also reflected in Shakespeare – the old values and codes of chivalry, like 'friendship' and 'honour' are presented in shifting arguments and contradictions. They are simultaneously used by a noble 'old-fashioned' character like Othello and a cruel opportunist like Iago, thus shifting their connotations and meaning in a clash of old traditions and new political realism.[129]

Yet many of Shakespeare's plays – especially the earlier comedies and tragedies – carry unmistakable signs of the post civil war period in their *abhorrence of rebellion and disorder*[130] and naturally embed the Elizabethan belief in a divine order of things. Nevertheless, the fates of *Macbeth* or *Richard II* serve as good examples for this defence of a godly order too, even if it is reinstated by force and rebellion. In this sense Shakespeare has also been interpreted as a forerunner of the Stuart civil war mentality, foreshadowing the trial and execution of James' son Charles I.[131] Elisabeth herself seemed to have felt this kind of foreshadowing in her hesitation to let *Richard II* be displayed on London's stages in the climate of the 1590ies crisis. She was skilled enough in staging herself, her trust and affection for her people – see the *Tilbury Speech* – to recognize the dangers of such a display of abdication by force.[132] Even if it is certainly not to be proven if Shakespeare had a wish to replace his queen, when staging *Richard II.*, the Essex coup, as well as the play, represents a kind of breakdown of the chivalric code and renaissance courtier manners in their attempt on rebellion against a rightful monarch. The indication that an unjust ruler may be successfully overthrown by his subjects should have been a frightening perspective for all ruling monarchs, not alone the ageing Elisabeth.[133] Shakespeare's rise to fame during the most troubled times of her reign in the 1590ies, times of political and social protest and a

---

[129] Joughin, John J.; *Shakespeare and Politics: An Introduction.*; pp. 3
[130] Coyle, Martin; *Shakespeare: Theatrical and Historical Contexts*; pp. 17
[131] Coyle, Martin; *Shakespeare: Theatrical and Historical Contexts*; pp. 19
[132] Coyle, Martin; *Shakespeare: Theatrical and Historical Contexts*; pp. 23
[133] Wilson, Richard; *Shakespeare in Hate. Performing the Virgin Queen.*; pp. 195

decline of royal authority, might have added to his turning to revolutionary themes.[134]

In his treatment of monarchy, some critics also re-evoke the *two bodies*[135] of royal authority, that have been described before – the common and the inaccessible. The elevation beyond the scope of mankind is nevertheless often followed by a downfall towards ordinary humanity, again to be observed in Macbeth or King Lear, but also in Elisabeth's last years of power.

Shakespeare's view of his queen is however highly debatable, the many legends describing her linking of him and his plays are strangely contradicted by his refusal to be involved in her glorification after she had died.[136] Yet she comes to life again as a character on stage in one of his later histories *Henry VIII* – staged after her death of course – as the resourceful and youthful maiden she certainly would have liked to stay in her subject's memories. During her time of reign Shakespeare did not openly name her or directly allude to her in any of his plays, which was of course due to the decree banishing the display of ruling monarchs, but still it is remarkable, for other playwrights like Ben Johnson were known to allude to Elisabeth directly in their plays, mostly under one of her associated 'personalities', like Cynthia or Belphoebe. During her last years her association with the moon was the most popular and widely acknowledged. The goddess of the moon served naturally as a symbol of virginity and immortality – the two aspects with which Elisabeth was best linked. The moon metaphors however were slightly unfortunate in their *comparing Elisabeth to the dark side of the moon*[137] and the embedded criticism. Even Hecate, the witch queen of *Macbeth*, is commonly associated with the dark moon. If, however, even statements like Theseus' *How slow this old moon wanes* (*A Midsummer Night's Dream* I,1) have a connection to Elisabeth – or the Treason Act of 1571,which made it illegal even to 'imagine' the queen's death – remains very debatable.[138] After all it

---

[134] Joughin, John J.; *Shakespeare and Politics: An Introduction.*; pp. 6
[135] Höfele, Andreas; "The Great Image of Authority". *Königsbilder in Shakespeare's Theatre.*; pp. 81
[136] see Wilson, Richard; *Shakespeare in Hate. Performing the Virgin Queen.*; pp. 150
[137] Wilson, Richard; *Shakespeare in Hate. Performing the Virgin Queen.*; pp. 160
[138] Wilson, Richard; *Shakespeare in Hate. Performing the Virgin Queen.*; pp. 163

can not be denied that Elisabeth's 'part' in *A Midsummer Night's Dream* is more widely believed to be Titania, whose love to an ass my be a slight criticism of Elisabeth's favours to her circle of young gentlemen, but who has no treacherous implications.

The presentation of English history and progress expired slowly under James' rule and became displaced by *Britain and Britishness* [139] as a sign of the imposed union of the nations. Theatre and plays were very popular, as has already been described, and not only King James hurried to choose his own theatre company; also his queen and sons patronized certain groups of players. If this patronage was a personal favour to Shakespeare or not, it constituted a protection of sorts against opposition and *In particular, royal protection enabled the privileged players to bypass restrictive municipal regulations [...]*.[140]

Consequently it is not surprising that far more allusions to King James can be found in Shakespeare's works than there can be certain allusions to Elisabeth – not taking into account the highly questionable method of connecting every mention of the moon to her. Yet it remains to be seen if Shakespeare's works really present evidence that conclusively hints at a propagandistic interest of King James in his theatre company. The fact that he needed propaganda perhaps even more than his predecessor, because of his lack of populism, meanwhile should be unquestioned.

James' conviction of the divine right to rule and his personal interest in literature presented him with a threefold self-concept: The *unifier* [141] of England and Scotland, a new Solomon or *philosopher-king* [142] and a new Augustus or *rex pacificus* [143] in Europe. He himself was not very successful in promoting these images, as could be seen in the historical abstract. Both court and parliament rejected his plans for a union with Scotland, his 'political poetry' was met with mistrust by his anti-absolutistic subjects and the peace in Europe was

---

[139] Wortham, Christopher. 1996. "Shakespeare, James I. and the Matter of Britain." In: Barry, Peter; Newton, Ken (eds.). *English. The Journal of the English Association*. Bangor, Wales: Bangor Univ. Press, Vol. 45. pp. 97-121.; pp. 97
[140] Wortham, Christopher; *Shakespeare, James I. and the Matter of Britain.*; pp. 99
[141] Wortham, Christopher; *Shakespeare, James I. and the Matter of Britain.*; pp. 102
[142] Wortham, Christopher; *Shakespeare, James I. and the Matter of Britain.*; pp. 104
[143] Wortham, Christopher; *Shakespeare, James I. and the Matter of Britain.*; pp. 105

not to be long-lasting in the struggles concerning power, commerce and religion.

Shakespeare and his company were asked more frequently to perform before the king than any other group of players - *from an average of just over three times a year during the last years of Elisabeth's reign to almost fourteen times a year.*[144] So even if King James did not see more theatre plays on average than Elisabeth, he certainly seems to have seen more Shakespeare plays. It seems natural therefore that Shakespeare would include some allusions to a king that patronized his company so graciously, no matter if he was personally connected with him in any way, and no matter if the king himself insisted on including some 'good publicity' in the plays or not. Consequently the character of King Lear for example is presented as the exemplified *King of Britain*[145] - a title James used for himself, but which was only an 'illusion covering an empty void', for it had no political weight in 17th century policy. King Lear's fate is as well to see his kingdom split in two by his greedy daughters and to witness its consequent downfall from alienation. King James should have applauded this prediction wholeheartedly.

Another example for events connected to King James in Shakespeare's plays is the fate of Macbeth, which shall be analysed in more detail later on. Contemporary literary criticism considered *Macbeth* to be an allusion to the Gunpowder Plot of 1605 – or in even wider connotation to the Darnley Murder, which indeed included a blown up building – and the king's escape from it. The basis for this linkage was the belief stated in *Macbeth* that the Stuart line would rule over England until the apocalypse, which in itself was a highly romanticised feature of 17th century belief. *Deliverance from the Gunpowder Plot was widely interpreted as manifestation of the divine will in fulfilment of the prophecies made in Revelation.*[146]

In consequence, the prophecies foreshadowing Macbeth's downfall and the escape of Fleance to father a new line of kings could be analysed in this context. Yet the witches and their prophecies may not have been such a timely topic of interest to the English people as they were to the Scottish. In James' time as King of Scotland there

---

[144] Wortham, Christopher; *Shakespeare, James I. and the Matter of Britain.*; pp. 107
[145] Wortham, Christopher; *Shakespeare, James I. and the Matter of Britain.*; pp. 110
[146] Wortham, Christopher; *Shakespeare, James I. and the Matter of Britain.*; pp. 114

had been – based own his own *Daemonology* – over 700 witch trials in only five years. None of them was as scandalous as the Countess of Essex' trial but a far greater number of people were burned alive in this short years than even in the same time under Bloody Mary's rule in England. When King James acceded to the English throne he made a habit of intervening in many witch trials, even if they were based on his own theories. This has been interpreted as a subtle, unobtrusive form of abandoning his own theories without official recognition of falsity.

In the next chapter of the essay the focus of argumentation will finally concentrate on some individual plays of Shakespeare, including of course the witch scenes of *Macbeth*, and it will be left to analyse if Shakespeare enthusiastically included more allusions to James and his work in *Macbeth* than the king would have liked[147], or if this was an equally subtle and unobtrusive form of criticising a monarch without being endangered by 'lèse-majesté'.

---

[147] Wortham, Christopher; *Shakespeare, James I. and the Matter of Britain.*; pp. 115

Shakespeare's Plays

Title page of the First Folio, 1623.
Copper engraving of Shakespeare by Martin Droeshout.

The Merchant of Venice

Among the problems one faces in dealing with The Merchant of Venice *is the difficulty of sensing a whole, a harmony, in a play that seems to work so consistently with dichotomies;*[148]

The Merchant of Venice has a long history of criticism and production throughout the centuries and has undergone countless reinterpretations accordingly. Many critics assume that of Shakespeare's plays only *Hamlet* has been enacted more often. The play itself evolved from a line of Shakespeare's earlier comedies and takes up themes from older productions, like the fairy tale setting of Belmont and the *disguised heroine*[149] already featured in *The Two Gentlemen of Verona*. However, the change of production style according to phenomenons of zeitgeist is especially important for this play.[150] From the 19th century onwards for example the change of presentation in the character of Shylock from villain to victim of the action is most noticeable – a similar development to the staging of *Macbeth*.

The Merchant of Venice is also the oldest of the plays that will be discussed in this second part of the essay and it is also the only one issued still under the reign of Queen Elisabeth. This is mainly due to the fact that Shakespeare's literary fame had increased immensely and importantly by his publication of the two poems dedicated to the Earl of Southampton in 1593. This, for the first time in his playwriting career, put him in a position to attain a partnership in the Lord Chamberlains Men in 1595 and, as has been shown before, probably forged a closer connection to the court.

---

[148] Benston, Alice N. 1979. "Portia, the Law and the Tripatite Structure Of the *Merchant of Venice*." In: Shakespeare Association of America. *Shakespeare Quarterly*. Washington D.C.: Folger Shakespeare Library, Vol. 30. pp. 367-385.; pp. 367

[149] Cerasano, S. pp. (ed.). 2004. *William Shakespeare's* The Merchant of Venice. *A Sourcebook*. London: Routledge.; pp. 2

[150] Puschmann-Nalenz, Barbara. 2006. "Nachwort." In: Puschmann-Nalenz, Barbara (ed.). *Shakespeare, William; The Merchant of Venice*. Stuttgart: Reclam.; pp. 195

Date and Source
The patron of this group, Lord Leicester, had died shortly after the defeat of the Armada but his stepson, the Earl of Essex, remained an important figure both for Elisabeth and the theatre. During the time of his most pronounced popularity among the people of London – namely the 'Raid of Cadiz' 1596 – most secondary sources estimate the first production of *The Merchant of Venice*.
The Andrew, a ship mentioned by Salerio in Act I[151] is supposed to represent the San Andrés, a ship captured by Essex during his campaign in Cadiz.[152] This establishes a first connection between the play and contemporary political developments and between the figure of Antonio and the person of Essex, for his venture to Cadiz was economically no more successful than most of Antonio's endeavours in the first part of the play.
Shakespeare's main inspiration for *The Merchant of Venice*, however, presumably derived form an Italian *novella*[153] by the name of *Il Pecorone* about 'Gianetto of Venice and the Lady of Belmont'. It is easy to see the connection of this story to the play, but nevertheless Shakespeare made several adjustments to fit it into the English renaissance society, so for example the casket plot was embedded into the wooing of Portia by her suitors. The idea of a golden, silver and lead casket may have come from the old *Gesta Romanum*[154], which had been revised and republished in England in 1595, and which provided a suitability test for brides-to-be in choosing between a golden, silver and lead vessel. This old Roman tradition was just perfect to replace the altogether more sexual indications of the original text, which would not have been tolerated by the London authorities. Nevertheless, it is not the suitability of the bride that is tested in *The Merchant of Venice* and it remains to be seen what indications this change bears concerning the situation of Portia and Queen Elisabeth. In addition, the change of dependency between Antonio and Bassanio also provides room for speculation,

---

[151] *And see my wealthy Andrew lock'd in sand [...]* (I,1,l. 27) All quotes from the primary text are taken from: Shakespeare, William. 1993. *The Merchant of Venice*. Cambridge: Cambridge Univ. Press.
[152] see i.a. Mahood, M. M. 1993. "Introduction." In: Mahood, M.M. (ed.). *Shakespeare, William; The Merchant of Venice; New Cambridge Shakespeare Ed.* Cambridge: Cambridge Univ. Press.; pp. 2
[153] Mahood, M. M.; *Introduction*; pp. 2
[154] Mahood, M. M.; *Introduction*; pp. 4

because it was changed from a godfather and godson to a 'mere' friendship. The bond plot of the original text between the merchant and the Jewish usurer remains however in place and it might have been the most attractive part for adoption in the political climate of the 1590ies. In 1594, the formerly Jewish royal physician Ruy Lopéz had been tried and executed for high treason. His charges were participation in a plot to poison Queen Elisabeth and collaboration with Spain. In the aftermath of this well-publicised trial, Christopher Marlowe's *Jew of Malta* was replayed several times with great success. It is probable therefore that Shakespeare wanted to capitalise on the timely anti-Jewish propaganda, as *[...]* The Merchant of Venice *offers, through its characterization of Shylock, one of the most dangerous instances of cultural stereotype [...]*[155]
Nevertheless, it has to be stated that the small community of converted Jews in London was, if not well respected, not completely outcast from the London society either. The fact that Dr. Lopez had long been the queen's physician and that Queen Elisabeth even had a formerly Jewish lady-in-waiting[156] proves that. It has also to be recognized that Marlowe's Barrabas, as the Jew of Malta, has much more in common with the alleged traitor Lopéz than Shylock – Barrabas, i.e., is a converted Jew and a prisoner. A definite change is also recognizable in the relation of the Jew and his daughter. While Abigail is happy to help her father and steal money *for* him, Jessica steals money *from* her father and is therefore abandoned. It will be analysed later on if this change could have some background in English history too.

Plot and Structure
The Merchant of Venice presents reader and audience with continuing contrasts and surprising combinations, like Venice and Belmont or Love and Money. On the whole it can not be denied that it must be considered a *romantic play*[157] about the power of friendship or the triumph of love. This fairy tale atmosphere Shakespeare conserved perfectly in plays like *A Midsummer Night's*

---
[155] Smith, Peter J. 1998. "Characterization and Stereotype: Theatrical Convention in *The Merchant of Venice*." In: Lascombes, André (ed.). *Tudor Theatre: Let There Be Covenents...*. Bern: Peter Lang. pp. 255-270.; pp. 264
[156] see Mahood, M. M.; *Introduction*; pp. 19
[157] Mahood, M. M.; *Introduction*; pp. 9

Dream is however disturbed by the realistic background of merchandise, ventures and financial enterprise in Venice. Of course, the Venice setting was already suggested in the original novella, but there also was a small community of Venetian merchants in London to provide the audience with some background information about the place. It is sometimes even suggested that these merchants were used as spies on the continent, for example by the Earl of Essex.[158]

At the time The Merchant of Venice *was written, the Republic was a legend for her independence, wealth, art, and political stability, her respect for law, and her toleration of foreigners.*[159]

These legendary virtues of the Italian republic were in fact already crumbling in the Elizabethan Age but her popularity was yet untarnished by political reality. The rise of middle class merchants and capitalism in the Elizabethan England is mirrored in Shakespeare's Venice, as are the nautical society, the dependence on foreign trade and the public masques and festivals. Nevertheless, the luxury and commerce of the Italian city creates an atmosphere of superficial friendship and insignificant pastimes, exemplified by funny but shallow characters like Gratiano. Shylock and his daughter also are ideally placed in the ghetto of Venice, as by a decree issued under King Edward I in 1290 no Jews were permitted to live in England that had not converted to Christianity.[160]

In addition to that exotic and somewhat illusory setting, the background of the English theatre history provides the influence of mediaeval morality plays that is visible in the cruel and infidel nature of Shylock or in Portia's demeanour as *advocatus dei*[161], the bringer of mercy and justice in the trial scene. It must, however, be stated that the mutual hatred shown by Shylock and Antonio makes it difficult to project common villain-victim profiles on the trial scene. In a strict Christian setting, Antonio's rejection of the infidel would have been fitting – his business with him and his lack of missionary Christian charity would not. The trial scene thus presents the

---

[158] Mahood, M. M.; *Introduction*; pp. 12

[159] Mahood, M. M.; *Introduction*; pp. 13

[160] see Baker, Elliot. 1995. "The Queens Hand in the *Merchant of Venice*." In: Goldstein, Gary B. (ed.). *The Elizabethan Review*. Middle Village, NY: Goldstein Press, Vol. 3. pp. 21-31.; pp. 21

[161] Mahood, M. M.; *Introduction*; pp. 10

murderous appetite of Shylock and opposes it, not with Antonio's, but with Portia's Christian grace and mercy.[162]

This concept of equity as a legal equivalent of mercy was highly common in renaissance England, as was the unifying aspect of Portia's intervention: The exact wording of the bond and thus the law is secured which does explicitly not exclude that mercy is procured in the conversion of Shylock, his only way to salvation.[163] This union of law and mercy was a utopian state that the law courts and the royal courts of Chancery tried and failed to achieve in their coexistence in London. The frequent use of trial scenes and judicial proceedings in Elizabethan plays suggest already a strong interest in these matters at the time *The Merchant of Venice* was written. Yet the trial scene in *The Merchant of Venice* is nevertheless unusual for its almost improbable outcome that is not even foreseen by the Duke. In addition to that, the 3000 ducats offered by Bassanio to win Antonio's freedom would have represented an almost surreal fortune in Elizabethan London and were supposedly meant to stress the fathomless wealth of Venice. It can however be assumed that these improbabilities would not have registered negatively with the English audiences as the far away setting of Venice provides enough distance to the English society and proceedings of court. It may even be possible that Shakespeare chose his trial as a critique on Venetian or English judicial processes. *The fleshbound plot in* The Merchant of Venice *helps to illustrate, in concrete terms, the 'interchangeability' of money and human flesh.*[164]

The opposing parties in the play, however, remain somewhat unclear. The marriage of Bassanio and Portia is presented from the first scene as the main goal of the whole romance plot and yet has the same sense of artificialness that lingers constantly behind almost every relation in the play. In the first encounter with Shylock – the assumed villain – Bassanio thus accepts Antonio's light-hearted sacrifice without a second thought to pursue his personal gain and Portia likewise is presented in a twofold way – the respectable demure face she turns to her suitors is only a disguise for her true feelings towards them, as she seeks a husband to release her from her

---

[162] Puschmann-Nalenz, Barbara; *Nachwort*; pp. 216
[163] see Mahood, M. M.; *Introduction*; pp. 18
[164] Cerasano, S. pp. (ed.); *William Shakespeare's* The Merchant of Venice. *A Sourcebook.*; pp. 19

father's will.[165] In this world of love and money Antonio and Shylock are both outsiders, set apart, misunderstood and even manipulated by their surroundings. But this factor does not unite them, for as Antonio's mood turns to separation and self-sacrifice, Shylock becomes bitter and cruel. Apart from this difference of character there is also an economic rivalry between Antonio and Shylock, yet in the trial scene it is not Antonio that struggles against the Jew's wish to kill him. Instead it is Portia that plays the counterpart to Shylock in this crucial part of the play, even although it can not be denied that she enters into a kind of rivalry with Antonio too, as far as Bassanio's love is concerned.[166]

All of these antagonisms have there own places and character combinations in Venice and Belmont. The hierarchy however between the Venice and Belmont scenes remains equally uncertain, as both setting have their main- and subplots to develop – Jessica's elopement, Lancelot and his father, the ring-plot, etc.

It also remains inexplicit who the actual main character of the play is. The first character to appear is Antonio, but he is sparsely defined beyond his label of *royal merchant*[167] - a strange definition nevertheless for an Italian republic. Portia on the other hand is not only fair and rich but also described as witty and capricious[168] - phrases highly reminiscent of Queen Elisabeth in her younger years. The casket-plot casts a more friendly light upon her personality as the somewhat cruel mocking of her former suitors. In her 'quest' for Bassanio she exemplifies both the will to obey her father and her insistence to take her own judgement into account, so as not to be won like a prize at gambling. This consideration of her as *a warmly and resourceful human person*[169] could be the basis for an interpretation with Portia at the centre of actions, for she combines the two main themes of the play: Love and Money. The 'give and hazard' aspect of the casket in which her picture is to be found is represented not only in Bassanio's relation to her, but also his

---

[165] see Moody, A. D. 1981 [4th repr.]. *Shakespeare. The Merchant of Venice.* London: Arnold Ldt.; pp. 23

[166] see Puschmann-Nalenz, Barbara; *Nachwort*; pp. 197

[167] Puschmann-Nalenz, Barbara; *Nachwort*; pp. 199

[168] *Puschmann-Nalenz, Barbara; Nachwort;* pp. 204

[169] Moody, A. D.; *Shakespeare. The Merchant of Venice.*; pp. 37

friendship to Antonio, to whom he is bound *in money and in love* .[170] This again stresses her opposition to Antonio and the strange unity of love and money, observed also in Shylock's and Lorenzo's relation to Jessica.

On the whole, the play can be summarized as a *play of movements*[171]: The action moves from Venice to Belmont to present the contrast of Antonio and Portia with Bassanio as the linking figure and the elopement of Jessica and Lorenzo as a counterexample to this match. The fates of the protagonists move from loss to gain as the meanings of hazard, risk, business, win and loss are elaborated both with connections to merchandise and love. Some characters move between trials and masques – Jessica and Portia dress as men, while Shylock, Bassanio and Gratiano are 'tried' by justice and love. And, finally, the relations of characters move from love to betrayal as Bassanio gives away Portia's ring, Jessica steals from her father and Lorenzo quarrels with her about the inviolability of love. Nevertheless, all these disturbances and activities – except Shylock and the trial scene – are dominated by a light-hearted tone that suffuses the seriousness of the discussed topics.

The confrontation of Venice and Belmont, Antonio and Portia and even Shylock and Portia represent the clashes of merchandise and love, justice and mercy, loss and gain, and reality and illusion.

---

[170] I,1, 130
[171] Mahood, M. M.; *Introduction*; pp. 25

Merchants and Jews

> The Jew was the scapegoat of Christendom and the usurer the scapegoat of nascent capitalism.[172]

On entering the first scene of *The Merchant of Venice* the topics of merchandise and risk are instantly palpable in the encounter of Antonio and his friends.[173]
The rise of the merchant class in England and the ensuing changes in society have been mentioned before and so it is not astonishing that Antonio seems to be a noble character, maybe even an aristocrat. His noble standing may have been soothing for Shakespeare's higher class of audiences, for even during the change of feudal systems, a greater permeability of social classes and the rise of lawyers to the highest circles of court, many a courtier still sought a kind of justification for his bourgeois business.[174] Aristocratic adventurers like Sir Walter Raleigh greatly helped to do away with these last strands of the mediaeval class system, even if they consequently suffered the losses and risks of the sea trade.

> *Hath all his ventures fail'd? What, not one hit?/ From Tripolis, from Mexico and England, / From Lisbon, Barbary, and India, / And not one vessel scape the dreadful touch / Of merchant-marrying rocks?* (III, 2, 266-69)

Consequently to this beginning the topic of finance or 'value' – both in a material and a mental meaning – remains one of the main themes of the play. The strange union of love and money mentioned before again and again casts doubts upon the moral standards of Shakespeare's protagonists. Perhaps it is therefore that *no other Shakespeare comedy at all, has exited comparable controversy.*[175]
In this sense the role of the usurer in the play serves as an example for the darker side of the rising capitalism in England and presents

---

[172] Mahood, M. M.; *Introduction*; pp. 21

[173] *Believe me, sir, had I such venture forth / The better part of my affections would / Be with my hopes abroad. (I, 1, 15-17)*

[174] *I know Antonio / Is sad to think upon his merchandise. (I, 1, 39-40)*

[175] Cohen, Walter. 1982. "*The Merchant of Venice* and the Possibilities of Historical Criticism." In: Ferguson, Frances (ed.). *English Literary History*. Baltimore, Maryland: Johns Hopkins Univ. Press, Vol. 49. pp. 765-785.; pp. 767

the counterexample to the hard-working Puritan ideal of self-reliance. The usurer, as opposed to the risking, hazarding merchant, relies on the work of others to make him rich, while not feeling compelled to help the poor and needing.[176]
Antonio in this sense appears next to Shylock as the chivalric hero of the play even though in reality the differences between usurers and merchants were often blurred, as are the boundaries of love and money in the play.[177] In the Elizabethan England of the 1590ies there was therefore issued a campaign against usury, openly supported by many courtiers and noblemen, who were not adept in adjusting to the decline of feudal bonds and thus had accumulated huge debts.[178]

>How much I have disabled mine estate / By something showing a more swelling port / Than my faint means would grant continuance: (I, 1, 122-24)

It is therefore probable that Shakespeare intended to present his Venice as a slightly contorted mirror of the English society, for *Venetian reality contradicted almost point for point its portrayal in the play.*[179] Shylock appears in the midst of all this change and bustle as an almost irrational, archaic, medieval character[180] whose downfall serves as a defence of the permeable English society over the old continental mediaeval feudal system – the *foundation of English monarchy*.[181]
That Elisabeth's finance experts, and so presumably she herself, was of the opinion that sound state finance equalled a secure and stable monarchy has been exemplified before. In *The Merchant of Venice*, it is Portia who expresses a similar idea, which anew stresses their strong likelihood: *Since you are dear bought, I will love you dear.*[182]
It is, however, not only Portia, whose character shall be discussed in

---

[176] *I oft deliver'd from his forfeitures / Many that have at times made moan to me, / Therefore he hates me.* (III, 3, 22-24)

[177] *A lady richly left [...] and she is fair, and, [...] Of wondrous virtues,* (I, 1, 160-62)

[178] Cohen, Walter. 1982. *"The Merchant of Venice* and the Possibilities of Historical Criticism."; pp. 768

[179] Cohen, Walter. 1982. *"The Merchant of Venice* and the Possibilities of Historical Criticism."; pp. 770

[180] see Cohen, Walter; The Merchant of Venice *and the Possibilities of Historical Criticism.*; pp. 771

[181] Cohen, Walter. 1982. *"The Merchant of Venice* and the Possibilities of Historical Criticism."; pp. 772

[182] III, 2, 312

the next chapter that links the play to contemporary renaissance rulers. Already the first lines of the play, spoken by Antonio, feel highly reminiscent of a later ruler of England – James VI of Scotland.
In sooth I do not know why I am so sad, / It wearies me, you say it wearies you; (I, 1, 1-2)
This sadness of Antonio seems throughout the play strangely motiveless and unfocussed, not even lifting completely in the end scene of rejoicing and reunion. Some critics have linked this moody demeanour to his outsider's position in Venice, misunderstood by his friends, left by Bassanio: *His passive demand for a deeper understanding and friendship meets no response.*[183] This would of course be an internal explanation as far as the text is concerned. Yet another more historical explanation could be found in the end of the Elizabethan era and the upcoming melancholy of the beginning 17th century, of which James was a perfect example.[184]
James mental instability and his tendency to extremely excessive and extremely sombre moods and the before mentioned fashionable infatuation with apocalyptic prophecies under his reign are signs of that melancholic and disturbed mood. *The Merchant of Venice* was certainly performed before James in 1605[185], but it is not apparent whether Antonio's 'motiveless melancholy' was added in the later productions, or if Shakespeare sensed the changing moods of society even in the 1590ies.[186]
Another important topic both for the play and the Elizabethan policy is of course religion. It has to be stated clearly, nevertheless, that Shakespeare on the whole was not concerned frequently with problems of belief[187], although some of his plays naturally feature old biblical archetypes. The Venice setting of the play would also impede a strictly religious interpretation of the text, as the city serves

---

[183] Moody, A. D.; *Shakespeare. The Merchant of Venice.*; pp. 21
[184] Maurer, Michael; *Eine kleine Geschichte Englands*; pp. 166
[185] Steele, Mary Susan. 1968 [repr.]. *Plays & Masques at Court During the Reigns of Elisabeth, James and Charles.* New York: Russel&Russel.; pp. 140
[186] *A stage, where every man must play a part, / And mine a sad one.* (I, 1, 78-79)
[187] Klause, John. 2003. "Catholic and Protestant, Jesuit and Jew: Historical Religion in *The Merchant of Venice.*" In: Taylor, Denis; Beauregard, David N. (eds.). *Shakespeare and the Culture of Christianity in Early Modern England.* New York, NY: Fordham Upp. pp. 180-221.; pp. 66

as an example for humanist ideals and capitalist interests: *[...] men for whom money is the most important thing are unlikely to go on crusades.*[188]
Religious allusions are, however, found in *The Merchant of Venice* and not only in the trial scene too– which many critics interpret as the confrontation of New (Portia) and Old Testament (Shylock). Portia's religious devotion is particularly established in the change Shakespeare included in Act IV, where he altered her destination to a monastery, instead of the health spa of the original Italian version.[189] The salvation of the *infidel* Jessica[190] and the *kind of devil* Shylock[191] represents is of course another highly Christian topic pursued throughout the text.[192]
As the confrontation of religions was however not a feature of the original novella[193] and as Jews were banned from England since the middle ages one has to consider the possibility that this topic might have been directed at the divided Christianity of Shakespeare's England.[194]
The sometimes alleged Jesuit influence on Shakespeare's works[195] would then put him into opposition to the Elizabethan Settlement? This would mean that Portia and the other Christian characters – especially perhaps Antonio, who could serve as a *martyr in mind and almost in the flesh*[196] - would have to be seen in a militant Puritan light, the oppressors of religious freedom. Ironic statements like Antonio's – *Content in faith, I'll seal to such a bond, / And say there is much kindness in the Jew*[197] – thus get a whole new dimension. To see the English Catholics represented by Shylock and the people of Venice as the English Protestants that have to learn their own laws,

---

[188] Bloom, Allan. 1964. *Shakespeare's Politics*. Chicago: Univ. of Chicago Press.; pp. 16
[189] see Klause, John; *Catholic and Protestant, Jesuit and Jew*; pp. 67
[190] III, 2, 217
[191] II, 2, 18
[192] *I shall be saved by my husband; he hath made me a Christian.* (III, 5, 15)
[193] Klause, John; *Catholic and Protestant, Jesuit and Jew*; pp. 69
[194] *I will buy with you, sell with you [...] but I will not eat with you, drink with you, nor pray with you.* (I, 3, 28-30).
[195] Klause, John; *Catholic and Protestant, Jesuit and Jew*; pp. 72
[196] Klause, John; *Catholic and Protestant, Jesuit and Jew*; pp. 90
[197] I, 3, 145-46

would definitely serve as a critique, perhaps not against the Settlement, but against the increasing control and deviation of Catholic minority since the death of Mary Stuart.

The absence of Jews in England since the reign of King Edward I did, however, only refer to Jews that would not convert to stay.

Nevertheless, *The most generous estimate of the number of Jews in the entire county has been less than one hundred.*[198] It is therefore questionable if the famous 'Jew-Speech' of Shylock[199] could indeed be interpreted as a defence of Judaism, unless Shakespeare had a particular Jew in mind. But why would Shakespeare write a defence of Ruy Lopéz that would contradict the contemporary political feelings?[200]

Dr. Lopéz had been the physician of Leicester and the queen's spy Walsingham before he entered her service. During the time he was part of the Leicester household, however, he was unfortunately involved in the scandal around the death of Amy Robsard, the Earl of Leicester's first wife. Yet this did not tarnish his reputation for long and he entered into the queen's service in 1586. To live in England, Lopéz had to be a Christian at least officially, which links him to Barrabas more than to Shylock. There is, however, a possible allusion to him in the trial scene: *[...] Thy currish spirit / Govern'd a wolf, who hanged for human slaughter.*[201]

Lopéz of course means wolf and indeed he was executed. It has been said that Elisabeth's favourite the Earl of Essex, had a personal grudge against him and pursued his conviction – whether this was due to the fact, however, that Lopéz reported to the queen the earl's infection with syphilis can not be conclusively proven.[202] In the end, Lopéz was arrested and shown into the torture chambers of the Tower, although not tortured himself. Nevertheless, the prospect should have been sufficient to result in a confession.[203]

---

[198] Baker, Elliot; *The Queens Hand in the* Merchant of Venice.; pp. 21
[199] III; 1, 46-53
[200] Baker, Elliot; *The Queens Hand in the* Merchant of Venice.; . pp. 22
[201] IV, 1, 133-34
[202] Baker, Elliot; *The Queens Hand in the* Merchant of Venice.; pp. 26
[203] *Ay, but I fear you speak upon the rack / where men enforced do speak any thing.* (III, 2, 32-33)

It is questionable if Shakespeare really included the speech of Shylock because of a royal decree, as some critics suggest[204], or whether his persecution of the Jew that is governed by mercy in the form of Portia did not evolve from a certain subjective mistrust against the Earl of Essex and his accusations:

> *If it be proved against an alien / That by direct, or indirect attempts / He seek the life of any citizen [...] the offender's life lies in the mercy / Of the Duke only, 'gainst all other voice.* (IV, 1, 345-52)

This charge of course greatly resembles that of Ruy Lopéz, and had Shakespeare really acted upon Queen Elisabeth's wish – for *All indications are that she never believed Lopez guilty.*[205] – or pursued a personal desire to dampen Essex's triumph, he would have placed his art completely in her service.

---

[204] see Baker, Elliot; *The Queens Hand in the* Merchant of Venice.; pp. 29
[205] Baker, Elliot; *The Queens Hand in the* Merchant of Venice.; pp. 29

Portia and the Law

> In terms of plot structure, however, [...] the play's crucial figure is neither Antonio nor Shylock but Portia, since it is her attitude toward the law that is central for these trials.[206]

The last chapter tried to show how the characterisation and description of the Venetian mercantile society and its inhabitants may reflect the Elizabethan England and what implications this could involve. The main reason for choosing *The Merchant of Venice* as a topic for this essay lies, however, in the character of Portia and her before mentioned resemblance with the young Queen Elisabeth. As it has been indicated that the queen herself might have had an interest in the play because of the Essex – Lopéz background, it feels even more coherent to make this connection.

Already the first lines referring to Portia in the first scene of the play underline this direction:

> *Nor is the wide world ignorant of her worth, / For the four winds blow in from every coast / Renowned suitors [...]* (I, 1, 166-68)

And another of her suitors puts even more emphasis on this likelihood, taking in England's unique geographical and religious position:

> *The watery kingdom whose ambitious head / Spets in the face of heaven, is no bar / To stop the foreign spirits, but they come / As o'er a brook to see fair Portia.* (II, 7, 44-47)

It is not difficult to associate statements like this to the situation of Queen Elisabeth, her foreign suitors and her circle of wooing courtiers, and of course her determination to keep her kingdom independent from Rome. Thus, the feminist criticism considers the underlying theme of *The Merchant of Venice* to be *the* structure *of exchange itself which characterizes both the economic transactions of Venice and the love relationships forget at Belmont.*[207]

---

[206] Benston, Alice N.; *Portia, the Law and the Tripatite Structure Of* The Merchant of Venice.; pp. 370

[207] Newman, Karen. 2004. "Portia's Ring: Unruly Women and Structures of Exchange in *The Merchant of Venice.*" In: Cerasano, S. pp. (ed.). *William Shakespeare's The Merchant of Venice. A Sourcebook.* London: Routledge. pp. 84-

The meaning of exchange in these circumstances is mostly a romantic or even sexual one. The casket-plot that links Portia to Bassanio, Bassanio to Antonio and Antonio to Shylock and the ring-plot in which a ring is given from Portia to Bassanio, back to Portia disguised as Balthazar, to Antonio, and back to Bassanio, have in this sense been interpreted as a description or even criticism of the Elizabethan love relationships or courtly 'manners'. Elisabeth and her circle of noble admirers certainly recalls Portia and her suitors, especially in her first appearance on stage in Act I scene 2. As has been mentioned before, the satirical depiction of political enemies of the queen was not persecuted by the Stationer's Office and so it is not astonishing that some suitors slated by Portia are highly reminiscent of Elisabeth's. So for example the 'French Lord'[208] reminds in her description strongly of the Duke of Alençon, Elisabeth's last foreign suitor, who had visited her in England in 1579 and whom she called her 'frog'.[209]

Morocco and especially Aragon on the other hand are clearly meant to resemble Spanish noblemen, perhaps even King Phillip himself, as his aunt Queen Catherine had been a Princess of Aragon. Their characterisations fall in with the common anti-Spanish feelings of the war times: dark and moorish, arrogant, pompous and foolish.[210] *For an Elizabethan audience this is the only way to describe a Spaniard.*[211]

And yet Portia's choice of a husband is impeded, as was Elisabeth's, by handicaps laid out by their fathers – for Portia the casket test and for Elisabeth the reason of state:

[...] in the fashion to choose me husband , - O me the word "choose" [...] so is the will of a living daughter curb'd by the will of a dead father: (I, 2, 18-21)

But as it turned out – and was unquestioned by the time Shakespeare wrote *The Merchant of Venice* – Elisabeth would not marry and lose

---

86.; pp. 85
[208] *[...] if a throstle sing, he falls straight a-cap'ring,*(I, 2, 49-50)
[209] Suerbaum, Ulrich; *Das elisabethanische Zeitalter;* pp. 187
[210] *"Who chooseth me shall have as much as he deserves"!/ Did I deserve no more than a fools head?* (II, 9, 57-58).
[211] Smith, Peter J.; *Characterization and Stereotype: Theatrical Convention in* The Merchant of Venice.; pp. 267

her independence of power.[212] She, like Portia, is portrayed as a woman who will take on male responsibilities and – even worse – is seen in public to handle them well.[213]
Her comment upon having to dress up as men to be able to win Antonio's trial [214] thus gets a sarcastic edge that would probably have greatly amused Queen Elisabeth, who often referred to her supposed lack of strength and her weaker sex in connection to her power, for example in the *Tilbury Speech*, and even the young and fair Portia seems to carry some of Elisabeth's severity of age and power: *[...] my little body is aweary of this great world.*[215]
Portia's reference to Diana, the moon-goddess, links her even more to the Virgin Queen, and this reference is taken up again in her return to Belmont:

> *Come ho! And wake Diana with a hymn, / with sweetest touches pierce your mistress' ear, / And draw her home with music.* (V, 1, 66-68)

Here in this last scene, the utopian aspect of Portia's domain is underlined, the unifying aspect of her presence that has already been encountered in the trial scene, which combines the *outer and inner wealth*[216] of her circle of friends. In this light it feels safe to assume, that the moon-reference made by Lorenzo can be interpreted as a flattery of 'The Lady of Belmont' or the Queen of England.[217]
With Portia, the Queen of Belmont returns to her native pastoral domain, having solved all problems forged in the bustle of the city of Venice – Antonio's trial, Bassanio's debt and Jessica's heritage. Portia's and Bassanio's marriage certainly reflects upon the changing Elizabethan class system and the transforming hierarchy in marriages, as Bassanio is, socially and economically speaking, a bad match for her and she definitely is no demure and obedient wife to him. Still the play comes up with *the romantic solution for a social*

---

[212] *I will die as chaste as Diana, unless I be obtained by the manner of my father's will [...]* (I, 2, 87-88)
[213] Newman, Karen; *Portia's Ring.*; pp. 85
[214] *They shall think we are accomplished / With what we lack;* (III, 4, 61-62)
[215] I, 2, 1-2
[216] Cohen, Walter; The Merchant of Venice *and the Possibilities of Historical Criticism.*; pp. 776
[217] *When the moon shone we did not see the candle. – So doth the greater glory dim the less, - / A substitute shines brightly as a king / Until a king be by, and then his state / Empires itself [...]* (V, 1, 92-96)

problem.[218] Bassanio as the only of her suitors was able to value her beyond her treasures: *So may the outward shows be least themselves; / the world is still deceived with ornament.* (III, 2, 73-74) This criticism of the superficiality of the cult around Portia could of course easily be applied to the Elisabeth cult as well.

Concerning this fairy tale ending some critics recall the contrast between town and country also visible in the English renaissance society, the rising self-esteem shown by the merchants of Venice and London, and the absolutistic tendencies already palpable in the forthcoming succession of James I.[219] If this, however, can be considered as a shadow of pre-civil-war mentality is highly questionable.

But of course Portia's true importance to the play lies in her intervention in the trial scene and her insistence of mercy as a counterpart to Shylocks insistence of revenge:

The quality of mercy [...] droppeth as the gentle rain from heaven [...] it becomes / The throned monarch better than his crown. [...] The attribute to awe and majesty, [...] It is enthroned in the heart of kings, (IV, 1, 180-90)

It has been said before that the plot of *The Merchant of Venice* evolves from movement, but one could also apply the structuring element of a *series of* three *trials*[220]: The casket-plot with its three caskets, the trial of Antonio which affects the three couples and the ring-plot with, including Jessica's ring, its three rings and Portia as the main figure around all these 'trials' evolve. Bassanio enters the contract of the ring equally light-hearted as Antonio enters his flesh-bond. By rescuing Antonio, Portia indeed also intervenes in favour of her own marriage, for the bond between Bassanio and Antonio would never be broken if she allowed Antonio to pursue his martyrdom. Yet by teaching them both the nature of mercy and forgiveness, her 'rule' is re-established in the end. As far as her struggle with Shylock is concerned, she also teaches him that who has no mercy for others, can not expect forgiveness in return. This is

---

[218] Cohen, Walter; The Merchant of Venice *and the Possibilities of Historical Criticism.*; pp. 778

[219] see Cohen, Walter; The Merchant of Venice *and the Possibilities of Historical Criticism.*; pp. 177

[220] Benston, Alice N.; *Portia, the Law and the Tripatite Structure Of* The Merchant of Venice.; pp. 369

the application of the same 'justice' or 'golden rule' before evoked by Shylock himself. Portia in her role as bringer of justice gains an almost divine post by revealing this hubris in the Jew[221] and to remind him that nobody is free from sin. This brings us back to Elisabeth's alleged intervention for her physician Lopéz; for Shylock's *greater guilt is that he would use the state's judicial system for purposes of private revenge.*[222] Essex' personal grudge against Lopéz and the ensuing trial could be found in this statement.

Another female figure that shall be discussed briefly in this chapter for her resemblance to renaissance rulers is Shylock's daughter Jessica. As has been elaborated before, Shakespeare changed the father–daughter relation in his play, compared to *The Jew of Malta*. This gives Jessica the opportunity to utter some phrases that are in some way reminiscent of Elisabeth's Catholic sister Mary I: Her rejection of a father that had lost the true faith[223], her abandonment under his rule[224], her grief at the divorce and banishment of her mother by her untrue husband and her own accusations of bastardy.[225]

These connections could of course be called far-fetched but as Shakespeare is again and again supposed to have supported the Catholic resistance in the 1590ies, and as the link between *The Merchant of Venice* and criticism of religious oppression has already been made in the last chapter, it feels necessary to reflect upon the fact that Jessica bears some resemblances to Mary. It is true that Tubal casts some doubts upon her character when he tells Shylock that his daughter has sold his treasured ring for a monkey, but even this assertion does not make her an unsympathetic character, as the constant suspicion of vanity and superficiality lingers over all Venetians in the play. Yet the elopement of Jessica and her lover Lorenzo seems on first glance to contradict the comparison of Jessica and Mary, as Mary's marriage was so desolate. However, the doubts

---

[221] *What judgement shall I dread, doing no wrong?* (IV, 1, 89)

[222] Benston, Alice N.; *Portia, the Law and the Tripatite Structure Of* The Merchant of Venice.; pp. 378

[223] *Alack, what heinous sin it is in me / To be ashamed to be my father's child!* (II, 3, 15-16)

[224] *I have a father, you a daughter, lost.* (II, 5, 55)

[225] *That were a kind of bastard hope indeed, - so the sins of my mother should be visited upon me.* (III, 5, 10-11)

she casts upon Lorenzo's honesty in the last scene of the play and the list of unhappy, even tragic couples preceding it, brings the connection back again:

> *In such a night / Did young Lorenzo swear he loved her well / Stealing her soul with many vows of faith, / And ne'er a true one.* (V, 1, 17-19)

In addition to that, the topic of unrequited love would not have been unknown to Queen Elisabeth in the climate of the 1590ies too, as her quarrels with her favourite Essex grew ever more wearisome. After his desperate campaign in Ireland and his exile from the court it is told that...

> *When the eights Muse approached Elisabeth [...] in a masque 1600 [...] and declared she was Affection,* "Affection *said the Queen, is false".*[226]

---

[226] Wilson, Richard; *Shakespeare in Hate. Performing the Virgin Queen.*; pp. 158

Macbeth

> *A knowledge of James' opinion of usurping tyrants has led to an interpretation of* Macbeth *as a study in tyranny: The King's interest in daemonology [...] to consider* Macbeth *as Shakespeare's contribution on the debate on witchcraft and necromancy.*[227]

As already indicated in the introduction, *Macbeth* is not usually counted among the 'Problem-Plays'. On the one hand, this might be due to the fact that all other plays discussed in this essay hover somewhere between comedy and tragedy, while in the case of *Macbeth* there can hardly be any doubt about its tragic nature. On the other hand, however, the distinction becomes more difficult when looking at the immanent structure of the play and its characters. One can not help but notice that this last of the four 'great tragedies' stands in some way apart from earlier works such as *Othello* or *Hamlet*. Some critics see this as an accomplishment of Shakespeare's tragic style and capability[228] - others note the complete strangeness[229] of the play in comparison to earlier *and* later works of Shakespeare, which in itself provides one of the aspects that define a 'Problem-Play'.

Nevertheless, of course some strands of Shakespeare's earlier works reappear in *Macbeth*, such as the hired murderers seen in *Anthony and Cleopatra*, the *mother's blood and milk*[230] theme from *Coriolanus*, or 'human' aspects of villainy followed by remorse, or supernatural influences, seen already in Hamlet and his father's ghost. Unlike *Hamlet*, however, the play seems far more dynamic

---

[227] Jack, Jane H. 1955. "*Macbeth, King James* and the *Bible*." In: Norris, Edward T. (ed.). *English Literary History*. Baltimore, Maryland: Johns Hopkins Univ. Press, Vol. 22. pp. 173-193.; pp. 175

[228] *In that play Shakespeare's final style appears for the first time completely formed [...]* Bradley, A. C. 1994 [rev. ed.]. "*Macbeth*." In: Wain, John (ed.). *Shakespeare Macbeth. A Casebook*. Houndmills: Macmillan. pp. 105-139.; pp. 105

[229] Rohjan-Deyk, Barbara. 1996. "Nachwort." In: Rohjan-Deyk, Barbara (ed.). *Shakespeare, William; Macbeth*. Stuttgart: Reclam.; pp. 200

[230] Braunmueller, A.R. 2007. "Introduction" In: Braunmueller, A.R. (ed.). *Shakespeare, William; Macbeth; New Cambridge Shakespeare Ed.* Cambridge: Cambridge Univ. Press.; pp. 6

and the characters involved do not get time to dwell on reasoning and planning. The darkness in which almost the whole action is placed – night, storms, shadows – underlines this immanent atmosphere of tumult and 'unreason'. The leitmotif of blood and confusion creates an image of a disturbed country full of haunted minds.[231] This feeling is even emphasised by the rash succession of short scenes and the dense, all but chaotic dynamics of the play – which remains one of the shortest plays Shakespeare has ever written – mixing verse, prose and linguistic styles.

Date and Source
Although court records are strangely unable to tell[232], it is widely assumed that *Macbeth* was written and performed first for King James and his brother-in-law, King Christian of Demark, during his visit in 1606.[233]
Thus, in a play written for court performance[234] it is not surprising that Shakespeare took to elaborating some themes of Scottish history to involve his patron's native country and noble ancestry in the action. As a king highly bent on defending his divine right to succession, especially in England, James was very interested in his royal heritage. In addition to this, the prejudices against Scotland and its inhabitants were still strong in the opposition to James and his court. *[...] hostility to James and his Scottish entourage spread from court gossip and the theatre [...]*[235]
The main source for the story of King Duncan and Macbeth can be found in Raphael Holinshed's *Chronicles*[236], a historical work that was republished in London in 1587 and whose second volume presents the *Historie of Scotland*. The there mentioned Banquo,

---

[231] Bradley, A. C.; *Macbeth.*; pp. 107
[232] see Steele, Mary Susan; *Plays & Masques at Court During the Reigns of Elisabeth, James and Charles.*
[233] see i.a. Wortham, Christopher; *Shakespeare, James I. and the Matter of Britain.*; pp. 111
[234] That *Macbeth* was written specifically for a performance at court before King James cannot be doubted in the light of the voluminous evidence [...] Ribner, Irving. 1953. "Political Doctrine in *Macbeth*." In: Shakespeare Association of America. *Shakespeare Quarterly*. Washington D.C.: Folger Shakespeare Library, Vol. 4. pp. 202-206.; pp. 202
[235] Braunmueller, A.R.; *Introduction'*; pp. 13
[236] Braunmueller, A.R.; *Introduction'*; pp. 13

Thane of Lochaber and friend of Macbeth, was widely believed to have based the line of Stuart kings, and it is therefore not surprising that in Shakespeare's play Macbeth's historical accomplice and his son Fleance take no part in any action – not in the murder of Duncan and not in the battle against Macbeth either. Indeed, in contrast to Macbeth, Banquo is described as wise and noble and his innocence may even be a cause for jealousy in the haunted Macbeth, whose attempts on self-improvement are perverted and inhuman. The latter's honour and grace remains to be seen only through their loss and absence.[237]

In Holinshed, the wife of the thane of Donwald – a loyal subject to King Duff – encourages him to murder the king, which he does, and to hide his body in a riverbed. Constant troubles, natural disturbances and signs of witchcraft are encountered by the new king until the body of King Duff is discovered. Macbeth himself, nevertheless, is described as a good, but hard ruler, reminiscent of King Henry VIII, who ruled Scotland for many years, eventually killing his accomplice Banquo, for fear he might try to murder him as they had murdered King Duncan. However, Macbeth's trust in witches and wizards is accounted for in Holinshed, as are the events of Birnham Wood. The legend of King Kenneth killing King Duff's son, to ensure his own line of succession, and suffering from insomnia from then on, can be found in Holinshed too, but to a far more detailed extent in the second source Shakespeare supposedly used, George Buchanan's *Rerum Scotiarum Historica.*[238]

Buchanan had been tutor to the young King James and it is therefore likely that the king was familiar with his works. The succession of Duncan, Macbeth and Malcolm are elaborated to reflect the Scottish transition form elected to inherited kingship and the play thus present the patterns of fatherhood, motherhood and unpredicted anomalies (untimely birth, infertility) in a political meaning of royal succession. The uncertainty of succession that had haunted the English society for decades under Queen Elisabeth's rule should have made this a highly attractive consideration for an Elizabethan and Jacobean audience too.

Other indicators for the time the play was written are the before mentioned Gunpowder Plot and the mention of a contemporary ship,

---

[237] Rohjan-Deyk, Barbara ; *Nachwort*; pp. 220
[238] Braunmueller, A.R.; *Introduction'*; pp. 15

like in *The Merchant of Venice*. The conspirators of the Gunpowder Plot were charged and executed for high treason in 1606, including one Father Henry Garnet, a Jesuit superior, who had published a pamphlet on religious equivocation and – as is widely believed[239] – is mentioned in the Porter scene:

Faith, here's an equivocator, that could swear in both the scales against either scale; who committed treason enough for God's sake, (II, 3, 7-8)[240]

Besides that, the *Tiger*, a trade ship, returned to London in the summer of 1606 and relayed the story of a most troubled journey to the public. In *Macbeth*, this serves as an example for the shipwrecking powers and petty revenges of witches, when the wife of a sailor refuses one of the witches some chestnuts: *Her husband's to Aleppo gone, master o'th Tiger: / But in sieve I'll thither sail [...]*[241]

The topics of witches and witchcraft might be strange to modern audiences.[242] But to a Jacobean environment they were not only real, but highly threatening.

The bible associated witches with treason[243] and instructed any faithful Christian to destroy their powers – even by murder. Therefore, in the tense political and social atmosphere of the 1590ies witch-trials had been increasing both in England and Scotland, although the level of hysteria never reached the peak of continental witch-hunts. In England, witches were traditionally seen as old, unsupported women, who communicated with certain 'familiars' – rats, cats, toads or flies – and who caused local crop failures, infertility or impotence of neighbours, or mysterious deaths of domestic animals. They were hardly ever charged with homicide. King James, however, was supposed to be influenced by the continental witch-trials, probably through his wife or tutors. He described the sexual pact with the devil or daemons, the witch

---

[239] see i.a. Braunmueller, A.R.; *Introduction*'; pp. 5

[240] All quotes from the primary text are taken from: Shakespeare, William. 2007. *Macbeth*. Cambridge: Cambridge Univ. Press.

[241] I, 3, 6-8

[242] *For most audiences of* Macbeth, *the ideas of witchcraft [...] are incomprehensible, repellent, temporarily 'foreign', and even alien.* Braunmueller, A.R.; *Introduction*'; pp. 29

[243] Braunmueller, A.R.; *Introduction*'; pp. 29

Sabbath, the black mass including the use of dead bodies, unbaptized children or baptized animals, and the powers of witches to create fog, fly through the air, spread disease, or sail in sieves over great distances.[244]
He also included their power of foreseeing the future and their ability to lure other people into darkness and evil with lies and treacherous prophecies. In consequence to their abnormality, witches were also believed to forego all signs of femininity and to be infertile, similar to Lady Macbeth, who allies with dark spirits to lose her sex and become cruel and unfeeling.[245] The major themes *darkness, sleep, raptness and confusion*[246] are exemplified in this pact, changing the nature of witchcraft from a local and petty, to a national and universal threat. It must be said, however, that Macbeth and his wife render themselves to the witches out of their own free will and fascination[247] and seem to welcome the raptness and darkness that cover their deeds.[248] In this they differ from other 'victims' of supernatural influences as shall be described later.

Plot and Structure
One of the most notable aspects of the structure of Macbeth is the almost total absence of comic relief. While other famous tragedies like *Romeo and Juliet* or *Hamlet*, beside their tragic outcome, still 'take the time' to amuse the audience with word plays or ridiculous characters, *Macbeth* effectively hones the ironic comedy of Iago to perfection.
A *'Sophoclean irony' by which a speaker is made to use words bearing to the audience [...] a further and ominous sense [...].*[249] Even the short and somewhat out of place looking entrance of the porter bears the feeling of a bad omen, a reminder of the Hell's Porter of medieval morality or mystery plays.[250] Also absent from most of the

---
[244] *Infected be the air, on which they ride;* (IV, 1, 137)
[245] see Braunmueller, A.R.; *Introduction*'; pp. 37
[246] Stirling, Brents. 1953. "The Unity of *Macbeth*." In: Shakespeare Association of America. *Shakespeare Quarterly*. Washington D.C.: Folger Shakespeare Library, Vol. 4. pp. 385-395.; pp. 385
[247] *You greet with present grace, and much prediction* (I, 3, 53)
[248] *Let light not see my black and deep desires;* (I, 4, 51)
[249] Bradley, A. C.; *Macbeth*.; pp. 111
[250] *If a man were Porter of Hell's Gate, he should have old turning the key [...] Who's there in the name of Beelzebub?* (II, 3, 1-3)

proceedings in the play is some kind of love story imbedded in other tragedies, even in *Hamlet*, though there to a sad and cruel extent. Yet the characters of Macbeth and Lady Macbeth remain rather limited in their ability to express feelings of love or affection in the rash and confused action of the play. There are some minor references that show that they provide a good match as far as their pride and ambition is concerned – even if they differ in the respects of cruelty and egoism – and the audience even gets a glimpse of their affection for each other, or at least what this affection had been like, before the disturbing events of the plot come into action.[251] But even if Macbeth and his lady might love each other desperately and tragically[252], still their human feelings of affection and love are not important in the action of *Macbeth*, where characters are reduced to the positions they hold in the political tragedy.

A notable factor of this political dimension of their relationship is, however, the strange reversal of abilities among them. While Macbeth seems to posses strength and power, but shows a complete lack of imagination in his horror after he has killed Duncan, his Lady dwells endlessly on the images of blood and death, without the power to act. Nevertheless, she remains the *grey eminence*[253] behind his throne until her mind is finally overwhelmed by the horrors it has created. In this sense it feels justified to see Macbeth as a play that involves the development of its characters[254], while other tragedies exemplified the unalterability of human nature, like Hamlet or Othello, who are not able to overcome their dispositions.

And yet some critics have tried to excuse Macbeth and his treachery by indicating his ability and fame as a soldier – the trauma of war and battle would serve as an explanation for Macbeth's inability to overcome his condition and to seek fulfilment of his desires outside the realms of murder and bloodshed.[255]

There has consequently been much disagreement on the 'quality' of Macbeth's villainy. Some critics have described him as a misled

---

[251] *This have I thought good to deliver thee (dearest partner of my greatness) that thou mightst not lose the dues of rejoicing, by being ignorant of what greatness is promised thee.* (I, 5, 9-11)
[252] Bradley, A. C.; *Macbeth.*; pp. 113
[253] Bradley, A. C.; *Macbeth.*; pp. 136
[254] Bradley, A. C.; *Macbeth.*; pp. 121
[255] *It will have blood, they say: blood will have blood:* (III, 4, 122) & Rohjan-Deyk, Barbara; *Nachwort*; pp. 203

hero, like Othello, while others see in his deeds *destruction for destructions sake*[256], a motivation similar to Iago's. His morality seems to steadily decline throughout the course of action, reversing the tradition of the morality play, and allowing his conscience to regain control of his actions only towards the end of Act IV.[257] Identification with such a character is made more difficult than it is with a flawed hero like Othello and perhaps only possible because we assume that some strength of moral feeling is still hidden under all the cruelty.

Moral values and standards of behaviour consequently are a major topic of *Macbeth*, albeit not in the superficial and worldly way of *The Merchant of Venice*. Evil supernatural powers in *Macbeth* seem to be a part of the world, although opposed to its divine order. The eternal battle, the cosmic fight, of Heaven and Hell is fought around the centre of human existence.[258] The confusion of illusion and reality is represented by the witches and their daemonic powers, which threatens the holy order and proclaim the reversal of all values:

> *[...] fight / Against the Churches; [...] Confound and swallow navigation up [...] bladed corn be lodged, and trees blown down [...] castles topple on their warders' heads [...] though the treasure / Of Nature's germens tumble all together,* (IV; 1, 51-58)

Yet although the play shows a battle between the forces of good and evil, the moral values transported by the action remain strangely focussed on detection and punishment, rather than higher meanings of mercy and grace. Macbeth wants to erase his remorse by eliminating his fear of enemies; he craves a peace of mind, for, unlike most villains, he was once a noble and moral character. However, his fear of detection and retribution remains firmly adjusted to this world and not the next, which would have presented another flaw in his character to any Anglican audience.[259]

---

[256] Heilman, Robert B. 1977. "The Criminal as Tragic Hero: Dramatic Methods." In: *Aspects of Macbeth. Articles Reprinted from* Shakespeare Survey. Cambridge: Cambridge Univ. Press. pp. 26-39.; pp. 26
[257] see Heilman, Robert B. 1977. "The Criminal as Tragic Hero: Dramatic Methods."; pp. 27
[258] Rohjan-Deyk, Barbara; *Nachwort*; pp. 202
[259] *[...] renown, and grace, is dead;* (II, 3, 87)

In addition to this, the eradication of opposition, does not decrease his fear of detection, but naturally even heightens his sense of vulnerability. Macbeth's tragic flaw or downfall thus does not end, but begin the play in his first murder of Duncan, the regicide that leaves him cursed, the villain of the play and unable to continue his common existence. He has not only slain his king, he has eliminated his ability to sleep and thus the ability to reasoned action.[260] Over and above this personal guilt, the murder becomes even sacrilegious by the stress put upon Duncan's grace and nobility of mind and by Macbeth's highly questionable justifications – in an Elizabethan or Jacobean sense the destruction of the holy order makes him even more villainous than the actual murder of a human being.[261]

After this horrifying incident, the years of Macbeth's reign described by Holinshed are condensed to mere moments by the rapturous succession of events and changes of scenery. Macbeth's sudden denomination as 'tyrant' after the banquet scene is not explained by any utterances of mistrust until this point.[262] After this initial mentioning of tyranny, however, the sufferings of his victims are more and more reflected upon the whole land, like in the case of Lady Macduff and her children.[263]

Nevertheless, the sheer monstrosity[264] of murdering a king and subjecting a whole nation to oppression and tyranny is in this case the disturbed and confused deed of an individual that in addition labours under supernatural evil influences.

This almost feels like a denial of reasonable organized opposition to a ruling monarch, which was supposed to have planned the Gunpowder Plot in 1605.

> *If th'assassination / Could trammel up the consequence [...] this even-handed justice / Commends th'ingredience of our poisoned chalice / To our own lips [...]* (I, 7, 2-12)

---

[260] see Stirling, Brents; *The Unity of* Macbeth.; pp. 386
[261] *[...] this Duncan / Hath borne his faculties so meek, hath been / So clear in his great office, that his virtues / Will plead like angels, trumpet-tongued, against / The deep damnation of his taking-off;* (I, 7, 16-20)
[262] *[...] and 'cause he failed / His presence at the tyrant's feast [...]* (III, 6, 21-22)
[263] *[...] that as swift blessing / May soon return to this our suffering country / Under a hand accursed!* (III, 6, 49-50)
[264] Rohjan-Deyk, Barbara; *Nachwort*; pp. 199

Macbeth and the Scottish Heredity

Before Macbeth English dramatists and their audiences generally understood Scotsmen as comical, alien, dangerous and uncivilized people – as Frenchmen, who spoke a form of English, perhaps.[265]

As was shown in the last chapter, *Macbeth* is – perhaps more than any other Shakespeare play – a political image of the Scottish origins and qualities of Stuart kingship. It feels therefore topically adequate to discuss it as the first of the plays written under King James' rule, even although the next play in line *Measure for Measure* was written earlier.

Macbeth essentially focuses on the Scottish history as relayed in Holinshed and James' own works, the *Daemonology* and the *Basilikon Doron*, to elaborate its political viewpoints. The original *Chronicles*, however, provided Shakespeare with a heredity *describing some round of violence, murder, rebellion and general turbulence*[266], in the realms of Scotland. This perception of his native country was well known to James, as it provided one of the most hindering aspects of his efforts to unite the British nations: Scottish history was so overburden with regicide and treason that the English parliament and court thought assimilation with such a nation dangerous to the king himself and the stability of succession.[267] It is therefore at least possible that Shakespeare wanted to conclude this dark image of Scottish heredity with the final victory of James' own lineage, the bringers of a new and brighter future.[268]

The Scotland of the beginning of *Macbeth*, however, is still engulfed in darkness and battle. Duncan and Macbeth represent the royal house of Macalpine, while the – most probably fictional – Banquo

---

[265] Braunmueller, A.R.; *Introduction'*; pp. 9

[266] Bradbook, Muriel. 1994 [rev. ed.]. "The Origins of *Macbeth*." In: Wain, John (ed.). *Shakespeare* Macbeth. *A Casebook*. Houndmills: Macmillan. pp. 236-258.; pp. 236

[267] Kinney, Arthur F. 1991. "Shakespeare's *Macbeth* and the Question of Nationalism." In: Newey, Vincent (ed.). *Literature and Nationalism*. Liverpool: Liverpool Univ. Press. pp. 56-76.; pp. 63

[268] Bleed, bleed poor country! / Great tyranny lay thou thy basis sure, (IV; 3, 31-32)

shall later father the line of Stewards, or Stuarts, the rulers of a new Scotland, foretold by the witches: *Lesser than Macbeth, and greater [...] Thou shalt get kings, though thou be none.*[269]
This Banquo is wise and noble, the worthy forebear of James, and sworn against Macbeth's treason, although he does not act against him.[270] It is part of the internal irony of the play that Macbeth creates new rulers of Scotland by trying to kill them – he kills Duncan, which makes his son seizes power, he kills Banquo, which makes his descendants Kings of Scotland in the years to come. It is therefore Banquo's murder that is presented as the turning point of the play, while the death of King Duncan is placed in a *location of secondary significance*[271], and Banquo's ghost that haunts Macbeth, as Duncan's lineage will seize to rule before long.[272]
It does no take much imagination to connect this kind of presentation of his noble ancestor to James' wish of ensuring his unquestioned right to rule in England. In contrast to the wise but passive Banquo, the heir of Duncan's line Malcolm thus exemplifies the flawed ruler, descendant of a declining line of mediaeval kings. His inadequacy to rule becomes obvious when he is unable to join the mourning of his dead father, the divine ruler, but thinks only of the advantage this death provides.[273] This proof of his disloyalty would have reminded Elisabeth's former subjects of the law introduced by her court that excluded any heir to the throne that had been involved in a plot to murder the former monarch. Malcolm technically is innocent of this deed, but a moral flaw still taints his character. Indeed in his encounter with Macduff he goes even further in his self-accusations and confesses that he is not able to think about the wealth and well-being of his subjects, but only to dwell on his own desires – the mark of a tyrant.[274]

---

[269] I, 3, 63-65
[270] In the great hand of God I stand; and thence / Against the undivulg'd pretence I fight / Of treasonous malice. (II, 3, 123-25)
[271] Williams, George Walton. 1982. "*Macbeth*: King James's Play." In: Roudané, Matthew C. (ed.). *South Atlantic Review*. Tuscaloosa, ALA. Georgia State Univ. Press, Vol. 47. pp. 12-21.; pp. 19
[272] [...] the worm, that's fled, / Hath nature that in time will venom breed, / No teeth for the present [...] (III, 4, 29-31)
[273] To show an unfelt sorrow is an office / Which the false man does easy [...] (II, 3, 129-30)

Macduff applies the label of tyrant – although indirectly – to this kind of rule too, yet he tries to defend Malcolm, perhaps out of desperation, for the ruling qualities, or indeed the existence, of Duncan's other son Donalbain are never mentioned again, and promises him: *Scotland has foisons to fill up your will [...]*[275]
Nevertheless, even Macduff can not deny that a tyranny as feared or planned by Malcolm would disrupt the holy order and taint the divine right to rule.[276]
The encounter of Macduff and Malcolm was also taken from Holinshed in essentials but extended by Shakespeare to a drastic level, which would have provided *to the royal auditor a proof of his wisdom*[277], a reminder that the takeover of the Stuart line in Scotland would have served a greater good, considering the alternatives. But although this careful flattery of the king was supposedly not missed by the court, Shakespeare did not forego the opportunity to contrast the archaic and confused realms of Scotland with the well-governed and peaceful English surroundings in which Malcolm and Macduff meet for their discussion of ideal kingship:

And here, from gracious England, have I offer / Of goodly thousands; but all for this, / When I shall tread upon the tyrant's head, / Or wear it on my sword [...] (IV, 3, 43-46)

Yet James was convinced of his mission to unify these two contradictory nations and keep the peace not only on his isle, but in the whole of Europe, for a peaceful era was supposed to proceed the apocalypse – which was desired and anticipated throughout the 17th century. This dedication to peacefulness of course meant a drastic change in the English realpolitik, and the decades of war that the last chapter of Elizabethan policy presented, were therefore quickly blackened to provide a triumph for the new regime: *BELLONA henceforth bound in Iron Bandes shall kiss the foot of mild triumphant PEACE [...]*[278] Macbeth is quickly associated with *that*

---

[274] *[...] but there's no bottom, none / In my voluptuousness [...] Boundless intemperance / In nature is a tyranny [...]* (IV, 3, 60-67)
[275] IV, 3, 73-88
[276] *Uproar the universal peace, confound / All unity on earth [...] If such a one be fit to govern, speak [...] Fit to govern? / No, not to live. – O nation miserable!* (IV, 3, 99-103)
[277] Bradbook, Muriel; *The Origins of* Macbeth.; pp. 239
[278] Kinney, Arthur F.; *Shakespeare's* Macbeth *and the Question of Nationalism.*; pp. 60

Bellona's bridegroom[279] to underline his bloody business as a soldier. That Bellona was also a favoured alter ego of Elisabeth during the war with Spain, can not be mistaken as coincidence, but as an example of how new regimes' propaganda often involves detraction of the old one. From the first scenes of the play it could in this context even be deduced that it actually was meant for a performance before the King of Denmark – who was King of Norway at that time as well:

Where the Norwegian banners flout the sky, / And fan our people cold. Norway himself, / With terrible numbers, / Assisted that most disloyal traitor [...] (I, 2, 49-52)

The memory of war between their states should have enhanced the glory of the contemporary peaceful and diplomatic rulers. The quality – and in effect also vitality – of a ruler would have been essential to a Jacobean audience, as the health and power of the monarch reflected in the Elizabethan world picture directly the health of the nation as a whole. Shakespeare was frequently referring to this sense of *body politic*[280], also expressed in a pamphlet written by King James, where he *referred to himself as 'the proper Physician of his Politicke-body' [...]*[281] Ironically, it is Malcolm, the flawed ruler, that lists the virtues of the divine ruler, to account for his inadequacy:

The king-becoming graces, / As Justice, Verity, Temp'rance, Stableness, / Bounty, Perseverance, Mercy, Lowliness / Devotion, Patience, Courage, Fortitude, (IV, 3, 91-94)

Only a rightful king, given the holy mission to rule a realm, had the power to bring health and peace to his kingdom. This conviction is also embedded in the belief that the rightful king had healing powers for diseases like scrofula, also known as The King's Evil.[282] Macbeth's *unholy rule*[283] was thus sure to infect the country, and in consequence the play's centrepiece is not Macbeth's triumph and coronation, but the gathering of his subjects and noblemen, which

---

[279] I, 2, 54

[280] Muir, Kenneth. 1977. "Image and Symbol in *Macbeth*." In: *Aspects of Macbeth. Articles Reprinted from Shakespeare Survey.* Cambridge: Cambridge Univ. Press. pp. 66-76.; pp. 69

[281] *A counterblast to Tobacco* as quoted in: Muir, Kenneth; *Image and Symbol in Macbeth.*; pp. 69

[282] *To the succeeding royalty he leaves, / The healing benediction [...]* (IV, 3, 157-58)

[283] Bradbook, Muriel; *The Origins of* Macbeth.; pp. 241

nevertheless turns out to be a *broken banquet or frustrated feast.*[284] Although in this scene no open mistrust against Macbeth's regime is directly voiced by his thanes and he is 'rescued' by his wife, the scene leaves a stain on Macbeth's reputation and his downfall begins. Shortly afterwards he is entitled tyrant and soon he has no followers left – or at least the audience does not get to see them – as he once more forces his country into war.[285]

James, stylising himself as bringer of peace and unifier of the nation, would thus have added another crime to Macbeth's heavy load of *wickedness of treason, of regicide and usurpation*[286] – the disturbance of the King's Peace. Duncan's description as gardener and shepherd of his noblemen reflects this kind of fatherly rule and protectiveness, expressed in James speeches too:

I am the husband and the whole Isle is my lawful wife; I am the Head; and it is my body; I am the Shepherd and it is my flock [...][287]

Macbeth might have had good intentions and might have been a fatherly, protecting character – the audience does not get to see it – but through the sacrilege of regicide he becomes the usurping tyrant and it is not in his power to rid himself of this guilt.[288]

James' English subjects welcomed the era of peace their new king was proclaiming, for the country had suffered immensely under the constant war expenses and taxes during Elisabeth's last year, yet *the idea of the Union of the Crowns, so beloved by James, was not universally favoured.*[289] In fact, a more central government would

---

[284] Williams, George Walton; Macbeth: *King James's Play.*; pp. 16

[285] *And that which should accompany old age, / As honour, love, obedience, troops of friends, / I must not look to have [...]* (V, 3, 24-26)

[286] Draper, John W. 1937-38. "*Macbeth* as a Compliment to *James I.*" In: Hoops, Johannes (ed.). *Englische Studien. Organ für englische Philologie unter Mitberücksichtigung des englischen Unterrichts auf höheren Stufen.* New York, NY: Johnson Reprint. Vol. 72. pp. 207-221.; pp. 218

[287] Kinney, Arthur F.; *Shakespeare's* Macbeth *and the Question of Nationalism.*; pp. 56

[288] *This tyrant, whose sole name blisters our tongues / Was once though honest: you have loved him well;* (IV, 3, 12-13)

[289] Kinney, Arthur F. 1993. "Scottish History, the Union of the Crowns, and The Issue of Right Rule: The Case of Shakespeare's *Macbeth.*" In: Brink, Jean R.; Gentrup, William F. (eds.). *Renaissance Culture in Context: Theory and Practice.* Aldershot: Scolar Press. pp. 18-53.; pp. 24

have had its benefits for both countries, as far as stability and efficiency of administration, trade and economy were concerned[290]; however, prejudices and fear of loosing privileges overruled such reasonable arguments – it was widely feared that the name and identity of England could be lost in favour of Scotland.

Yet the witches' prophecy in *Macbeth* seems to embed a kind of meta-level, when showing predictions of this kind of union preceding the apocalypse to their royal audience.[291] In this meta-level we can even discover similarities between Macbeth and James, as both are determined to build their regime upon a united kingdom.[292] In consequence, both are given a dire warning through the action of the play.[293]

The witches' prophecy does also include a show of the glory of Stuart succession imbedded in the apparitions the witches create for Macbeth, showing him the line of kings that will evolve from Banquo's lineage.[294] The problem of heredity, fatherhood and the unnaturalness of infertility is often brought up during the play to support Malcolm's claim to overthrow the tyrant – although it is hinted briefly that technically Macbeth is not an usurper, due to the still existing election system. Yet Macbeth grieves over his childlessness that will bring his efforts to procure the crown to nothing:

> *Upon my head they placed a fruitless crown, / And put a barren sceptre in my gripe, / Thence to be wrenched with unlineal hand, / No son of mine succeeding [...]* (III, 1, 62-65)

Although James continued Elisabeth's mystification of pre-marriage chastity – one thing he has in common with the unfortunate Malcolm:

> *[...] I am yet / Unknown to woman; never was foresworn; / Scarcely have coveted what was mine own; / At no time broke my faith [...]* (IV, 3, 125-28)

---

[290] Kinney, Arthur F.; *Shakespeare's* Macbeth *and the Question of Nationalism*.; pp. 57

[291] *Will the line stretch out to th'crack of doom? [...] And some I see, / That twofold balls and treble sceptres carry,* (IV, 1, 116-20)

[292] *As happy prologues to the swelling act, / Of the imperial theme [...]* (I, 3, 127-28)

[293] *A good and virtuous nature may recoil, / In an imperial charge [...]* (IV, 3, 19-20)

[294] *Show his eyes, and grieve his heart [...]* (IV, 1, 109)

This rather strong emphasis on the divine lineage of kings reflected of course King James' own conviction of divine royal succession. Indeed, after the tense political situation ensuing from Elisabeth's childlessness, and the scandalous behaviour of James' mother – including her role in the murder of Henry Darnley – stability and order were most craved by James' new subjects as well. James' pride in his descent from nine successive sovereigns[295] thus did meet the feeling of the time, even although by the decrees set in place by King Henry VIII, James was technically not allowed to take over the English crown, as Henry had banned all descendants of his sister Margaret from the heritage of England. This argument was silenced by the lack of alternatives and Queen Elisabeth's testament, but nevertheless it is not surprising that James sought to underline his right to rule and to stress his holy mission. *Kings, he declared "are not only GODS Lieutenants vpon earth [...] they are called Gods [...]*.[296]

Although this kind of absolutistic ideas were regarded with some mistrust by his English subjects, the conviction that abdicating a ruling monarch by force provided a serious breach in the divine order of things, was still widely anticipated, which for example the Earl of Essex discovered to his cost. Still James was – as Elisabeth had been – constantly on the lookout for rebellion and treachery, especially in the later years of pre-civil war animosity and disturbance.[297]

King Henry VIII regularly charged his courtiers with treason, Elisabeth established a quite effective espionage system, James relied on his divine status, but neither of them was unchallenged by the fear of rebellion and civil war.[298] *Macbeth* reflects upon that kind of fear in several passages, finding it both in the good and bad ruler. The fear of revolution serves thus as a uniting element between the usurper and the divine ruler, that ultimately leaves them the same fate as Macbeth – *a poor player, / That struts and frets his hour upon the stage, / And then is heard no more [...]*[299]

---

[295] Bradbook, Muriel; *The Origins of* Macbeth.; pp. 242

[296] Draper, John W.; Macbeth *as a Compliment to James I.*; pp. 213

[297]*To be thus is nothing, but to be safely thus:* (III, 1, 49-50)

[298]*This is the very painting of your fear: / This is the air-drawn dagger, [...]* (III, 4, 60-62)

[299]V, 5, 23-25

Thus another major topic reflected in *Macbeth* does present itself in the measures and justifications of governmental and royal control of opposition. Macbeth's measure to rid himself of the threat of Banquo and his descendants may in the play be explained by the soldier's cruelty dominating his conscience, yet the eradication of opposition and inconvenient pretenders is not a fictional event only.[300]
The general development in Europe during the 17th century turned from feudal, to absolutistic regimes – the only exception being England, where feudal bonds were replaced with democratic processes, as observed in the Elizabethan Settlement. The feudal system provided the king with all-but nominal power, whereas the absolutistic regimes suffered from the lingering suspicion of tyranny.[301]
In England, the personal power of the monarch had decreased palpably since King Henry VIII, who was also the last ruler of England unscrupulously crossing the line between keeping the peace and eradication opposition. In this light of democratic development, *Macbeth* appears to present the 'darker' side of absolutistic ideology, as an excuse for excessive violence. Already in the first scenes of the play a dangerous dependence of King Duncan on his best fighter is visible in the praise and promotion he gives Macbeth – *What he hath lost, noble Macbeth hath won.*[302] This situation is somewhat reminiscent of Elisabeth and her suspicions against her 'hero' Essex[303] and already suggests that Macbeth could easily turn his actual power into *full legal authority.*[304]
Where then lies the distinction between an absolutist monarch and a tyrant? The *Basilikon Doron* answers this question by denying any similarities between the two, stating boldly that no king who is not

---

[300] *[...] Things without all remedy / Should be without regard: what's done is done.* (III, 2, 11-12)

[301] *What does the tyrant? [...] He cannot buckle his distempered cause / Within the belt of rule.* (V, 2, 11-16)

[302] I, 2, 67

[303] *There's no art, / To find the mind's construction in the face:* (I, 4, 11-12)

[304] Sinfield, Alan. 1986. "*Macbeth*: history, ideology and intellectuals." In: MacCabe, Colin (ed.). *Critical Quarterly*. Ames, IA: Blackwell, Vol. 28. pp. 63-77.; pp. 65

an usurper, can possibly be a tyrant.[305] This makes the case of Macbeth not easier, as he technically is not a usurper.
Shakespeare compromises on stressing his inability, his alliance with evil and supernatural forces and the protest of nature against his rule.

> *[...] How did you dare, / To trade and traffic with Macbeth, / In riddles, and affairs of death [...] And, which is worse, all you have done / Hath been but for a wayward son,* (III, 5, 3-11)

The short time of Macbeth's rule in contrast to the original text also enhances that feeling of usurpation. James himself counted upon his divine, almost magical status among his subjects, although the mistrust against his absolutistic ambitions lead to dire accusations – for example that the discovery of the Gunpowder Plot was a fake, planned to provide the king with some sympathy and mystique.[306] It is certainly true that the Gunpowder Plot increased the strictness of measures taken by the government against such extremist forces. *Macbeth* as a play on rebellion and counter-rebellion naturally includes this contemporary issues: the measure of violence inflicted by the state, the right to resist a tyrant and the duty to serve the divine king.

Under the rightful rule of Duncan, a rebel and traitor like Macdonwald was sworn against the holy order of nature[307] During the course of the play Macbeth is consequently first promoted for striking down a rebel[308], and ends up with his own head upon the stake, reflecting the *instability of [...] authorized and unauthorized violence.*[309]

> *We'll have thee, as our rarer monsters are, / Painted upon a pole, and underwrit, / 'Here may you see the tyrant.'* (V, 8, 25-27)

---

[305] Sinfield, Alan. 1986. "*Macbeth*: history, ideology and intellectuals."; pp. 66
[306] see Kinney, Arthur F.; *Shakespeare's* Macbeth *and the Question of Nationalism*.; pp. 64
[307] *[...] The merciless Macdonwald / - worthy to be a rebel for to that / The multiplying villainies of nature / does swarm upon him - [...]* (I, 2, 9-12)
[308] *[...] with bloody execution [...] And fixed his head upon our battlements.* (I, 2, 18-23)
[309] Wilson, Richard. 2007. "Blood Will Have Blood: Regime Change in *Macbeth*." In: Deutsche Shakespeare-Gesellschaft. *Shakespeare Jahrbuch*. Bochum: Kamp Verlag, Vol. 143. pp. 11-35.; pp. 16

In addition to that, a traitor like Macdonwald is accredited martyr-like qualities[310], while Macduff leaves his wife and children to be slaughtered as innocent victims of this struggle for power and is ready to fight violence with violence.[311] There seems to be a distinction in *Macbeth between the violence which the State considers legitimate and that which it does not.*[312] Ambiguous characters like Macdonwald, Macduff, Malcolm and to some extent Macbeth[313] make it even harder to distinguish between 'justified' and 'criminal' violence. The warning of the witches does fit in here too: the borderline dividing oppression and order, violence and persecution, is to easily crossed in the search for 'imperial charges', or the 'greater good'. The last scene of the play does bring this difficult contrast to the present and implies again the union of nations intended by James.

Hail! King! For so thou art. Behold, where stands / Th'usurpers cursèd head [...] My Thanes and kinsmen / Henceforth be Earls [...] (V, 9, 21-30)

The question remains if *Macbeth* might thus be considered a flattery or a critique of James' political convictions and plans. As some critics point out, the political doctrine introduced in the course of the play might not reflect upon Shakespeare's own convictions, as it was so dangerous for Elizabethan and Jacobean authors to freely express views contradicting the authority.[314] Yet it remains to be concluded that Shakespeare put some consideration into the description of James ancestry and also provided careful justification for Macbeth's downfall. Nevertheless the dark side of absolutistic ideals, the thin line dividing the absolute monarch and the tyrant, even if blurred by Macbeth's 'obvious unnaturalness', would not have been included to please a monarch that was facing enough opposition to this kind of ideas already and whose own *Basilikon Doron* stated firmly that tyranny is *the greatest evil into which a king can fall.*[315] Here we may

---

[310] *Nothing in his life / Became him like him leaving it [...]* (I, 4, 7-8)

[311] see Sinfield, Alan; "*Macbeth*: history, ideology and intellectuals."; pp. 68

[312] Sinfield, Alan; "*Macbeth*: history, ideology and intellectuals."; pp. 63

[313] *Thou wouldst be great; / Art not without ambition, but without / The illness should attend it [...]* (I, 5, 16-18)

[314] see Ribner, Irving; *Political Doctrine in* Macbeth.; pp. 202

[315] Jack, Jane H.; Macbeth, *King James and the Bible*.; pp. 176

glimpse the author's anticipation and agenda through his work. However, the final evidence for this kind of conclusion – the reaction of court and king – are not to be reconstructed from the sources available. *The final political meaning of* Macbeth *[...] is not on the play, or in any performance of it, but well beyond the stage, in the palaces of Whitehall and Hampton Court.*[316]

---

[316] Kinney, Arthur F.; *Scottish History, the Union of the Crowns, and The Issue of Right Rule: The Case of Shakespeare's* Macbeth.; pp. 52

Witches and Daemons

In early modern England, witches and witchcraft were political matters as well as personal, familial, and communal ones.[317]

As has been mentioned before, the display of evil powers and witches was not frequently used in the Elizabethan and Jacobean theatre before *Macbeth*, yet the republishing of James' *Daemonology* and the more serious charges raised against witches under the continental influence, led surely to a greater interest in these matters throughout the country – and probably to a greater fear of these destructive forces, observed in the Overbury scandal.

Holinshed had included a strange apparition presenting itself to Macbeth in his *Chronicles*, describing *three women in strange apparel, resembling creatures from elder world.*[318] These apparitions were, however never called witches, although their demeanour would strongly suggest them to be supernatural. However, occult forces were not only associated with old hags but also with the hermetic circles and 'wizards' that had evolved from Christian mysticism and included high ranking courtiers. Even Queen Elisabeth favoured her 'court magician', Dr. Dee. Christopher Marlowe's *Faustus* reflects this image of a wise, clever, but misled genius, who wrought a pact with the devil. Witches, however, were not treated with this kind of fascinated respect. *While Dee or Forman consorted with kings and princes, the witch was generally a poor, solitary, ignorant, old woman.*[319]

The witch therefore did not seek higher learning about the nature of the world, but dwelled in petty mischief and revenge. Midwives, women skilled in herbal medicine and solitary living old women were often accused of witchcraft, including the brewing of love-potions, communication with spirits, foretelling the future and controlling the weather. However, the trial of the North Berwick Witches, *one of the most celebrated witch-trials of the age*[320],

---

[317] Braunmueller, A.R.; *Introduction*; pp. 29
[318] Holinshed'd *Chronicles* as quoted in: Draper, John W.; Macbeth *as a Compliment to James I.*; pp. 208
[319] Bradbook, Muriel; *The Origins of* Macbeth.; pp. 247
[320] Bradbook, Muriel; *The Origins of* Macbeth.; pp. 237

conducted by King James in his time in Scotland 1590 gave a new and more threatening dimension to the power and ambition of witchcraft.

All this Agnes Sampson and her coven claimed to do in their attempts to destroy the ship carrying King James from Denmark.[321]

The witches of Macbeth were clearly influenced by the North Berwick trials, for the protocols were widely published throughout the country and provided precedence for the politically motivated application of witchcraft, quite apart from personal or local effects.[322]

It must, however, be stated that the supernatural 'help' granted Macbeth is almost non-existent. Macbeth and his Lady are by no means given any powers equalling those of Dr. Faustus, no angels or daemons are involved on either side. In addition, Macbeth and his wife enter into the 'guidance' of the witches with almost suspicious eagerness and all dark deeds accumulated in their course of actions must therefore be regarded to be entirely their own. Thus they present living examples of the vileness and cruelty embedded in the human soul even without supernatural possession. If this, however, can be interpreted as a critique of the *Daemonology* is disputable, bearing in mind the political necessity of vilifying the tyrant and the importance of the witches as an argument for Macbeth's abdication.

King James' ensuing conviction from the encounters with the Berwick coven, expressed in the *Daemonology*, was that as the well-being of the monarch secured the wealth of the nation, evil forces would focus on the person of the ruler and become his worst enemy.[323] It was thus the holy mission of the king to rid his country of these evil powers and the sin of witchcraft and wizardry.[324]

Shakespeare's witches seem to have developed from the images of witchcraft developed by King James, rather then the traditional English ones. Both traditions were agreed, however, on the fact that a witch would be a woman and that several witches would form a

---

[321] Bradbook, Muriel; *The Origins of Macbeth.*; pp. 248

[322] *Shipwrecking storms and direful thunders, / So from that spring, whence comfort seemed to come, / Discomfort swells [...]* (I, 2, 26-28)

[323] see Jack, Jane H.; *Macbeth, King James and the Bible.*; pp. 175

[324] see Draper, John W.; *Macbeth as a Compliment to James I.*; pp. 208

coven or sisterhood – a perverted form of nunnery.[325] A coven of witches would then take to haunting a deserted landscape, like the blasted heath, and cause mischief and discomfort to people nearby or revenge themselves upon people who have offended them, disappearing into fog to avoid detection.[326]
But they were also able to evoke deep and dark desires in the people around them, increase their greed and hatred of each other, like Banquo discovered to his cost.[327] The control of the weather[328] and the travel by air[329] are also introduced in the appearance of the witches. The witches' dances were also recorded in the Berwick protocols:

The Weïrd Sisters, hand in hand, / Posters of the sea and land, [...] Thrice to thine, and thrice to mine, / And thrice again to make up nine (I, 3, 30-34)

But no record proved the ability of the captured witches to foresee the future.[330] The frequent use of body parts and children in the witches cauldrons were, however, recorded in the trial of Agnes Sampson and her fellow witches.[331]
In addition to the general reflections on witchcraft presented in the *Daemonology*, King James also issued a pamphlet concerned with the North Berwick trial in 1591 – *Newes from Scotland declaring the damnable life and death of Doctor Fian, a notable Sorcerer.*[332]
Doctor Fian – or John Cunningham – Agnes Sampson and her coven of witches were charged with high treason for plotting to murder the king. It must, however, be stated that all their confessions – some of them contradictory – were made under torture. Nevertheless, the

---

[325] *Where hast thou been, sister?* (I, 3, 1)
[326] *Into the air; and what seemed corporal / melted as breath into the wind [...]* (I, 3, 79-80)
[327] *And, prophesying with accents terrible / Of dire combustion, and confused events,* (II, 3, 49-50)
[328] *In thunder, lightning or in rain?* (I, 1, 2)
[329] *Hover through the fog and filthy air.* (I, 1, 12)
[330] Draper, John W.; Macbeth *as a Compliment to James I.*; pp. 211
[331] *Liver of blaspheming Jew [...] Nose of Turk, and Tartar's lips; / Finger of birth-strangled babe,* (IV, 1, 26-30)
[332] Calhoun, Howell V. 1942. "James I. And the Witch Scenes in *Macbeth.*" In: The Shakespeare Association of America. *The Shakespeare Association Bulletin.* New York, NY: Folger Shakespeare Library, Vol. 17. pp. 184-189.; pp. 184

pamphlet included the sacrilege of baptizing animals and *all that they together went bye Sea each one in a Riddle or Cive.*[333]
Only the witches' Sabbath, held to communicate with the devil, is in the play changed to an encounter with the witch queen Hecate – the dark goddess of the moon and counterpart to Diana, which we have encountered before.[334] This change of 'protocol' in the witches' Sabbath brings us back to the mention of Bellona and considerations of publicity, assuming for the sake of the argument Shakespeare's readiness to serve purposes of royal propaganda.

James had foreseen two major tasks in his accession: Overcoming his foreignness and *masculinizing*[335] the government that had been adjusted to Elisabeth's rule for 40 years. James had to carefully change this cult of virginity and femininity to a more suitable one of fraternity and paternal protectiveness. He still kept parts of the idealisation of chastity, but at the same time he had to emphasise strongly the security of his lineage, procured by his two sons and family.

This insurance of succession and promise of stability served as one of the strongest arguments for his new subjects to overcome their animosities against his Scottish descent. In the light of this changed perception of childlessness it is not surprising that causing infertility was counted amongst the many ways witches threatened the holy order of nature. Had childlessness under Elisabeth served as a sign of her special connection to her subjects, it now became a sign of unnaturalness, a *mark of demonic resistance*.[336] In consequence, Lady Macbeth's refusal to be a woman is a much more secure sign of her alliance with evil forces, than her role in Duncan's murder.[337]
Her strong character and steel-hearted ambition would in a Scottish setting not contradict her femininity, for it could have been

---

[333] *Newes from Scotland declaring the damnable life and death of Doctor Fian, a notable Sorcerer* as quoted in: Calhoun, Howell V.; *James I. And the Witch Scenes in* Macbeth.; pp. 188

[334] *Great business must be wrought ere noon. / Upon the corner of the moon* (III, 5, 22-23)

[335] Tiffany, Grace. 1996. "*Macbeth*, Paternity and the Anglicization of James I." In: Indiana University of Pennsylvania Faculty of Humanities. *Studies in the Humanities*. Bloomington: Indiana Univ. Press, Vol. 32. pp. 148-162.; pp. 148

[336] Tiffany, Grace. 1996. "*Macbeth*, Paternity and the Anglicization of James I."; pp. 149

[337] *Confusion now has made its masterpiece!* (II, 3, 59)

influenced by Scottish tradition where women were loving mothers and fearsome warriors.[338] Yet her infertility – or more accurately the assumed early death of her child or children – and her wish to be sexless, however, makes her almost a witch in her own right:

> *[...] Come you Spirits, / That tend on mortal thoughts, unsex me here, / And fill me, from the crown to the toe, top-full / Of direst cruelty! [...]* (I, 5, 38-41)

Feminist criticism sees this as evidence for the reversal of values in the regime change from Elisabeth to James, and indeed there are certain aspects that would suggest that a side-blow on the 'Fairy Queen' is intended in the witch queen of *Macbeth*.[339] The next step suggested by this line of criticism, however, that digests *Macbeth* as a play of male destructivity and the threat of female infertility – directed perhaps at Elisabeth and her favourites – should not necessarily be accounted for as royal propaganda. As James' right to rule still lay to a great part in the testament of Elisabeth and as she was preserved in the minds of her subjects as the bringer of a golden age, James should not probably have been interested in blackening her name directly, or present her as a threat to the kingdom post mortem. This would have caused nothing but 'bad publicity' on his behalf.

Yet it can not be denied that witches were often charged with bringing infertility and disruption to marriages and cause babies to be slaughtered. Macbeth's attempt to kill Banquo's sons and his slaughter of Macduff's children fits into this image. As has been mentioned before, the topics of fatherhood and heredity are central to the plot, making the eradication of Macduff's family more horrible and his 'betrayal' of them more serious:

> *His flight was madness: when our actions do not; / Our fears will make us traitors [...] to leave his wife, to leave his babes, / His mansion, and his titles in a place / From whence heself does fly? [...]* (IV, 2, 3-8)

This sequence is also somewhat reminiscent of another female figure in James' past – the flight of his mother Mary Stuart to England, leaving her husband Bothwell for good and her baby son to be raised by her enemies. Another aside to the fate of Mary Stuart could even be seen in the encounter of Macbeth and his three murderers – the

---

[338] see Bradbook, Muriel; *The Origins of* Macbeth.; pp. 245
[339] *And now about the cauldron sing, / Like elves and fairies in a ring,* (IV, 1, 41-42)

counterpart to the three witches – and his explanation why he needs others to kill Banquo:
> For certain friends that are both his and mine, / Whose loves I may not drop, but wail his fall / Who I myself struck down [...] (III, 1, 120-22)

Perhaps an Elizabethan audience would have thought of Elisabeth's desperate attempts to rid herself of Mary Stuart without signing the death sentence herself. Some critics even link the armed head and the bloody baby that arise out of the witches cauldron to a sighting of strange phenomenon on the day Mary Stuart was decapitated and *a bloodie head dancing in the air*[340] was seen in the streets of Edinburgh.

Visions and prophecies present another major theme of *Macbeth*, beginning with the fates of Banquo and Macbeth foretold by the witches. Banquo's prophecy is even important for the history of England and Scotland, while Macbeth's only becomes important for the play. Yet *[...] visions, omens, prophecies, and magic are often debatable, confusing, terrifying, inscrutable.*[341]

Like the vision of the flying dagger[342] taken from the Holinshed *Chronicles*[343] the visions of *Macbeth* exemplify the contorted nature and disturbing power of the witches, confusing values, virtues and desires. After the first prophecy of the witches Banquo reveals his wisdom and tries to bring back the lost sense of reason[344] and his justified mistrust,[345] while Macbeth struggles with his desires and his conscience.[346] He is in effect not able to overcome the lure of prophecy and falls for the false hope of greatness. *[...] because* Macbeth *is less a story of regicide and tyranny than of the war between the forces of evil and supernatural good.*[347] It is not

---

[340] Calhoun, Howell V.; *James I. And the Witch Scenes in* Macbeth.; pp. 188

[341] Kinney, Arthur F.; *Scottish History, the Union of the Crowns, and The Issue of Right Rule: The Case of Shakespeare's* Macbeth.; pp. 31

[342] *Is this a dagger, which I see before me [...] A dagger of the mind, a false creation, / Proceeding from the heat-oppressèd brain?* (II, 1, 38-39)

[343] Kinney, Arthur F.; *Scottish History, the Union of the Crowns, and The Issue of Right Rule: The Case of Shakespeare's* Macbeth.; pp. 32

[344] *Or have we taken the insane root, / That takes the reason prisoner?* (I, 3, 82-83)

[345] *What! can the Devil speak true?* (I, 3, 105)

[346] *This unnatural soliciting / Cannot be ill; cannot be good:* (I, 3, 120-30)

[347] Jack, Jane H.; Macbeth, *King James and the Bible*.; pp. 185

surprising in this rapt state of Macbeth that the prophetic warning of Banquo...
And oftentimes, to win us to our harm, The instruments of Darkness tell us truths; / Win us with honest trifles, to betray's / In deepest consequence. (I, 3, 122-25)
...falls on deaf ears.
As another example of Shakespeare's tragic irony it is maliciously chorused later by the witches[348] and their queen: *And you all know, security / Is mortals' chiefest enemy.*[349]
Macbeth's infatuation with his dreams of power and his determination to use any means to secure his crown[350] disrupt the nature around him, infect his wife and are laid down as the basis for his downfall. The natural order is disturbed[351] and Macbeth's mind is confused and unfocussed on reason and nobility.[352]
In all this incidents may be seen the careful justification Shakespeare provides for the murder of the king as opposed to the regicide of Duncan. The latter was a crime against the divine order of things, and all consequent measures taken to bring Macbeth down serve as readjustment of this holy right.
The play thus suggests that even nature must revolt against such usurpation, a similar propaganda to that of *Flavi et dissipati sunt.* Indeed for all its careful warning or anticipation of a tyrannical absolutism *Macbeth* is still a play full of Stuart policy and ideology, which needed all propaganda it could get in the rising tension between King James and his subjects.
I 'gin to weary of the sun, / And wish th'estate o'th'world were now undone. (V, 5, 48-49)

---

[348]*That this great King may kindly say, / Our duties did his welcome pay.* (IV, 1, 130-31)

[349]III, 5, 32-33

[350]*More shall they speak; for now I am bent to know, / By the worst means, the worst [...]* (III, 4, 134-35)

[351]*A falcon tow'ring in her pride of place, / Was by a mousing owl hawked at, and killed.* (II, 4, 12-13)

[352]*Nature seems dead, and wicked dreams abuse / The curtained sleep: Witchcraft celebrates / Pale Hecate's off'rings [...]* (II, 1, 50-53)

Measure for Measure

Measure for Measure *holds today an unassailable position as the chief "problem" among the various plays of Shakespeare [...]*[353]

The text of *Measure for Measure* presents, in contrast to *Macbeth*, no disagreement as far as its problematic nature is concerned. The play has been called strange, even alien to modern audiences.[354] The changing nature of the plays arguments, the character's dispositions and the general ambivalence of many a passage has made it rather hard to perform and difficult to analyse. Consequently it has been rediscovered as an interesting piece of Shakespeare's works only at the beginning of the 19th century, when noted literates like G.B. Shaw saw it as an example for Shakespeare's time-overlapping qualities.[355]
As a study of *system, trial and breakdown*[356] it has since then led to decade-long arguments, concerning the nature of the text, its ambiguous qualities and the purpose of its composure.
Developing *Measure for Measure*, Shakespeare leaned heavily on traditional folk tale motives, contemporary sources, and especially daily politics of the changeover from Elisabeth to James, rather than developing strands of his earlier work. Only the temporally abdication of Duke Vincentio resembles somewhat King Lear's decision to stand aside to rescue his kingdom. The setting of Vienna on the brink of battle with Hungary for example reflects on the contemporary tension between the English crown and the Habsburg emperor Rudolf[357] II, at that time King of Hungary.[358] The closure of the entertainment districts, brothels and theatres included in *Measure*

---

[353] Miles, Rosalind. 1976. *The Problem of Measure for Measure. A Historical Investigation.* London: Vision Press. pp. 1
[354] Pache, Walter. 2004. "Nachwort." In: Pache, Walter (ed.). *Shakespeare, William; Measure for Measure.* Stuttgart: Reclam.; pp. 227
[355] Pache, Walter. 2004. "Nachwort."; pp. 228
[356] Hawkes, Terence. 2004. "Take Me to Your Leda." In: Alexander, Catherine M. S. (ed.). *Shakespeare and Politics.* Cambridge: Cambridge Univ. Press. pp. 219-236.; pp. 220
[357]*Heaven grant us its peace, but no the King of Hungary's.* (I, 2, 4-5)
[358] All quotes from the primary text are taken from: Shakespeare, William. 2007 [updated ed.]. *Measure for Measure.* Cambridge: Cambridge Univ. Press.

for Measure had in addition just been lifted from London, as the public life flowed back to normality after the severe outbreak of plague during 1603.[359]
The general magnitude of different sources, combined of folk-tales, novellas, other contemporary plays and works of political theory makes it probable that Shakespeare had spend some time researching tales and inspirations during that time.[360]

Date and Source
The account of the Revels Master presents as date of the first court performance of *Measure for Measure* the 26th of December 1604, only a few months after James' accession to the throne of England.[361] The plot and characters are taken from various plays, folk-tales, and novellas and yet *Measure for Measure* differs from all of these sources in its focus on *retribution, mercy and justice*.[362]
Most critics assume that the title and its implications are taken from the bible – see for example Matthew 7.1-2: *Judge not that ye be not judged. [...] with what measure you mete, it will be measures to you again*.[363] – or the Sermon on the Mount. Yet such allusions had to be taken up carefully as the law forbidding staging living monarchs extended to religious sovereignty as well.
Still *Measure for Measure* shows some traces of the old feud between church and crown. The reversal of Christian virtues in Angelo's reign or the lax handling of moral during the Duke's reign thus stands in severe contrast to the Angelo's own, if hypocritical, insistence on piety and moral. *[...] as holders of office they forget the temporary nature of that power, the fact that power is not a Christian word*.[364]

---

[359] *All houses in the suburbs of Vienna must be plucked down.* (I, 2, 80)
[360] Pache, Walter; *Nachwort*; pp. 235
[361] Steele, Mary Susan; *Plays & Masques at Court During the Reigns of Elisabeth, James and Charles.*; pp. 140
[362] Gibbons, Brian. 2007 [updated ed.]. "Introduction." In: Gibbons, Brian (ed.). *Shakespeare, William; Measure for Measure; New Cambridge Shakespeare Ed.* Cambridge: Cambridge Univ. Press.; pp. 1
[363] Matthew 7.1-2 as quoted in: Gibbons, Brian; *Introduction;* pp. 1
[364] Gash, Anthony. 1998. "Shakespeare's Carnival and the Sacred: *The Winter's Tale* and *Measure for Measure.*" In: Knowles, Roland (ed.). *Shakespeare in Carnival.* Houndmill: Macmillan Press. pp.177-211.; pp. 200

Both examples relate to the Christian conviction that human desires stain the moral of men and a divine ruler should be focussed on avoiding lewd behaviour for the sake of his realm.[365] The Reformation had forged this close connection between private moral standards, official law, equity and Christian mercy throughout Elisabeth's reign, and it had become a common conviction in the public opinion of the beginning 17th century.[366]
The catholic setting of Vienna could, however, serve as a 'disguise' for a staging of English circumstances, as had Venice or Verona before. The allusions to English society are however palpable in the Puritan efforts to make fornication punishable by death and a desire for stricter moral education for children – voiced for example in Phillip Stubbe's *Anatomy of Abuses*[367], published during the 1580ies and by Duke Vincentio:

> We have strict statues and most biting laws [...] Which for this fourteen years we have let slip [...] so our decrees, / Dead to infliction, to themselves are dead, / And Liberty plucks Justice by the nose, / The baby beats the nurse [...] (I, 3, 19-31)

The counter-movement to this ascetic moral was also strong in London at that time, focussing on the hypocrisy supposed in the Puritan myth of abstinence and the holy arrogance of one flawed human towards others.[368]
Apart from these examples of daily policy and public debates, Shakespeare leaned on two major sources for his play – G.B. Giraldi Cinthio's novella *Hecatommithi* (1565) and George Whetstones play *Promos and Cassandra* (1578).[369]
Cinthio's novella is set in the realm of Innsbruck, which provides the Catholic surroundings of Maximilian – the Roman Emperor – and his trusted courtier Juriste, who is sent to rule Innsbruck in his

---

[365] *[...] I have delivered to Lord Angelo, / A man of stricture and firm abstinence, / My absolute power and place here in Vienna,* (I, 3, 12-14)
[366] see O'Harae, Alison. 2003. "Which Model? Whose Measure?: Sexuality, Morality and Power in *Measure for Measure* and *Basilicon Doron*." In: Chowdhury, Radhiah (ed.). *Philament Free Journal of Postgraduate Scholarshipp.* Vol. 1.
[367] Gibbons, Brian; *Introduction*; pp. 2
[368] *But man, proud man, / Dressed in a little brief authority [...] Plays such fantastic tricks before high heaven* (II, 2, 121-25)
[369] see Gibbons, Brian; *Introduction*; pp. 7-19

absence. Here again the source accounts for many years of good and just rule under the new sovereign, until Juriste is forced to sentence a young man for the rape of a lady. The young man's sister Eptia pleads for her brother – he is willing to marry the woman he has dishonoured. Yet this kind of equity is refused by Juriste unless Eptia surrenders to his lust for her. After Juriste's proposal to marry her in due course, Eptia is talked into accepting by her brother, despite her moral doubts. Eptia goes to Juriste, who has her brother executed anyway and sends her the severed head. Swearing bitter revenge, Eptia travels disguised to Maximilian's court and charges Juriste with raping a virgin. Juriste is made to plead for mercy before the emperor, while Eptia insists on having her revenge. Juriste is sentenced to marry her and then to be beheaded for his offence, but Eptia appeals to the emperor's mercy not to rid her of her new husband so violently. The story resolves in a happy ending, Juriste and Eptia being married and the emperor content in showing the mercy that suits the heart of princes.[370]

Cinthio's own adaptation of the tale for the stage also involved a hesitant captain, who saves Eptia's brother and so changes her motivation for pleading mercy for her husband.

On this stage adaptation Whetstone based his version *Promos and Cassandra* but included for the first time the feature of a long neglected law. He also changed the charge of rape to mutual engagement, giving the fiancée of Cassandra's brother an acting part, while letting the brother himself be sent to exile after his rescue from the scaffold to create a melodramatic effect in his return. This might have been the attraction for Shakespeare, who in his later works often sought the kind of *tragic-comedy*[371] embedded in *Measure for Measure*, while Whetstone apart from all melodrama still kept the unambiguous features of the traditional renaissance comedy.

The novella by Cinthio is thereby the basis of both plays, but Whetstone and Shakespeare elaborated the original story to their own purpose. Shakespeare in particular was interested in the action's heroine – changing her Shylock-like thirst for revenge to a virtuous quest for justice – and in the motivation of the deputy ruler, keeping the sexual implication, but contrasting it with a struggle for the

---

[370] *[...] I do think that you might pardon him, / And neither heaven nor man may grieve at the mercy.* (II, 2, 49-50)
[371] Gibbons, Brian; *Introduction*; pp. 11

upholding of justice. He also 'invented' the figure of the Duke and gave him the opportunity to voice significant parts of the *Basilikon Doron* – another topic of the public debate so shortly after King James accession.

Plot and Structure
The play *Measure for Measure* can be read and performed extremely ambiguous, due to its many possibilities of character and plot motivation.
The focus on men's free will and free choice of action towards good or evil is especially shown in the leitmotifs of liberty and restraint, justice and mercy, vice and virtue. Around these themes the ethic implications of morals, sexuality and human norms[372] centre.[373] Still many critics feel that there is a kind of *cynical pessimism*[374] in the presentation of the 'comedy' that makes a negative production much more likely than a romantic or comical one.
One of the major features in this play – also coming from the comedy background – is the use of disguises, already seen in *The Merchant of Venice*. The Duke's disguise serves as the central cause for the whole action and he is the figure controlling and motivating most of the plot.
It is remarkable, however, that this long lasting disguise of a male protagonist is a novelty in Shakespeare[375], whose female heroines – like Portia and Viola – disguise as a defence mechanism or out of opportunism. The motivation of the Duke, however, to leave his throne and roam the streets unnoticed, is often thought of as something like an autocratic measure[376]. His disguise *invades the privacy of his subjects*[377] and reminds the pessimistic reader of the espionage tactics used against the Catholic minority in the 1590ies.
The fear of rebellion and justification for his rule is especially apparent in the Duke's encounter with Lucio, who could either be regarded as the voice of rebellion or as a mirror reflecting the Duke's

---

[372] Pache, Walter; *Nachwort*; pp. 236
[373] *[...] for if our virtues / Did not go forth of us, 'twere all alike / As if we had them not.* (I, 1, 33-35)
[374] Miles, Rosalind; *The Problem of Measure for Measure.*; pp. 14
[375] see Miles, Rosalind; *The Problem of Measure for Measure.*; pp. 163
[376] Pache, Walter; *Nachwort*; pp. 237
[377] see O'Harae, Alison; *Which Model? Whose Measure?*; pp. 3

'real self'. This aspect of a concealed – and flawed – grey eminence[378] will certainly be an interesting feature when comparing Vincentio to King James.

Another topic to be examined is the nature of the disguise itself. As mentioned before, friars where no common features of the Jacobean society anymore and often regarded resentfully by the *common opinion*.[379] As with the Jew, the friar could therefore have some different implications that could register in the historical analysis.

In addition to the concealed authority of the Duke the audience gets the strict and inexperienced rule of Angelo, whose pride in ascetic temperance make him a perfect example for the Puritan hypocrite or the blueprint of the tyrant. A *Machivellian figure, who knew himself to well to care for anything else*[380], or in contrast a man contorted by power, whose self-image turns out to be self-delusion.[381]

His motivation to crave for Isabella is almost ironical, as only a woman of the same virtues he would like to posses can touch him.[382] Still his 'love' remains firmly based on sexual lust; the whole play lacks – as did *Macbeth* – a kind of romantic mutuality, only shown briefly by Juliet and Claudio. *Angelo's pharisaic pride and the static self-image [...] would impair his ability to approach [...] a love relationshipp.* [383]

Although Angelo is presented at the end of the play as the typical repented sinner, he is not, at the beginning, the typical hypocrite, for he is at no point a comic relief character. His self-delusion and pride is portrayed to give the Duke opportunity to conclude the justice and mercy motive at the end.[384]

The character of Isabella presents even more difficulties and some critics have called her Shakespeare's only *unlikeable*[385] heroine.

---

[378] see Miles, Rosalind; *The Problem of* Measure for Measure.; pp. 166
[379] Miles, Rosalind; *The Problem of* Measure for Measure.; pp. 169
[380] see O'Harae, Alison; *Which Model? Whose Measure?*; pp. 6
[381] *[...] Lord Angelo is precise [...] scarce confesses / That his blood flows; or that his appetite / Is more bread than stone. Hence shall we see / If power change purpose [...]* (I, 3, 53-55)
[382] *Dost thou desire her foully for those things / That make her good? [...]* (II, 2, 174-75)
[383] Miles, Rosalind; *The Problem of* Measure for Measure.; pp. 194
[384] *[...] Is this her fault, or mine? / The tempter, or the tempted, who sins most [...]* (II, 2, 163-64)
[385] Miles, Rosalind; *The Problem of* Measure for Measure.; pp. 214

Isabella's purpose in the course of actions seems to be to undergo a kind of forced education, similar perhaps to *The Taming of the Shrew*. Her role as a novice makes her as strange to the early Jacobean audience as the friars, but it could be seen as a justification of her otherwise cruel and merciless convictions of honour and redemption.[386]

The image of exchanging a sister for gain was, however, a common feature on the renaissance stage[387], but unlike other plays and tales Isabella is offered neither marriage nor money, she is not even threatened in any physical way. The 'only' thing to rescue would be her brother's life and many critics have seen her refusal to trade her honour for her brother's love as equally hypocritical as Angelo's proposal. In the end her pride is tested by her open charge on Angelo, even if Mariana relieves her of the public shame before long. Her virtuous arrogance thus evaporates in her last speech to save Angelo's life and Mariana's happiness, making her *more likeable here than she has been during the rest of the play.*[388]

The ambiguity of the play arises therefore mainly from the fact that it is focussed on elaborating the development – and in this case 'education' – of its characters. The beginning of the play presents us with three main characters, Vincentio, Angelo and Isabella, whose 'functions' are not defined and so it is not directly assailable where the reader's and audience's sympathy should lie. The audience would supposedly feel pity for minor characters like Claudio and his Juliet, the discarded Mariana, wise Escalus or the hesitant Provost.

Yet Shakespeare also presents figures like Barnadine and Lucio, who are almost as controversial as the main roles. The edification offered by the play – or the Duke – throughout the course of action clears some of these ambiguities in 'relieving' Angelo from his hypocrisy, Isabella from her virtuous arrogance, Claudio from his fear of death and finally the Duke from his reluctance to show himself to his people.

Only Lucio seems to be excluded from this merry purification in his protest to marry a whore. [389]

---

[386] *There is a vice that most I do abhor, / And most desire should meet the blow of justice; For which I would not plead, but that I must;* (II, 2, 29-31)
[387] Miles, Rosalind; *The Problem of* Measure for Measure.; pp. 220
[388] Miles, Rosalind; *The Problem of* Measure for Measure.; pp. 228
[389] Pache, Walter; *Nachwort*; pp. 252

The re-occurrence of the *Measure for Measure* reference in the last act...
The very mercy of the law cries out [...] An Angelo for Claudio, death for death [...] and measure still for measure.
(V, 1, 400-404)
...is thus sometimes accounted for as comic irony, preluding the Duke's final all-embracing justice or mercy. The silences of almost all 'convicted' characters, including Claudio, Juliet, most interestingly Isabella and Angelo and excluding again only Lucio – provide ample opportunity for most contrasting productions.[390]
A director could have Isabella turn away and grieve her destiny or celebrate her luck, Angelo to be disgusted by his fate[391] or show humble resignation. It is most probable that these staging possibilities of character silence were duly recognized by Shakespeare.

---

[390] *[...] and for your lovely sake / Give me your hand and say you will be mine [...] By this Lord Angelo perceives he's safe [...] Look that you love your wife: her worth, worth yours.* (V, 1, 484-90)
[391] *That I crave death more willingly than mercy.* (V, 1, 469)

Angelo, the Duke and the Ways of Power

> *The characters in* Measure for Measure *do not only use and resist arguments, they also become arguments themselves, inadvertently demonstrating certain truths about human nature, often while they are trying to achieve some quite different end.*[392]

During the time of changeover from Elisabeth to James, interest in his political treatise among James' new subjects was most pronounced, especially in *London's best-seller*[393] the *Basilikon Doron*. This was a new phenomenon in the English society as neither Elisabeth nor her father, as the two most important Tudor monarchs, had taken to elaborate their convictions in written from, rather than pronouncing them in public. Yet James' unwillingness to 'socialize' with the citizens of his capital presumably left them no other source of information about their new king.[394] The references to political discourse in *Measure for Measure* therefore are taken up already in the first lines, Shakespeare gave to Duke Vincentio:

> *Of government the properties to unfold / Would seem in me t'affect speech and discourse, / Since I am put to know that your own science / Exceeds, in that, the lists of all advice / My strength can give you [...]* (I, 1, 3-7)

Mostly it has been assumed, that this statement was directly given to the royal audience, serving as a careful flattery of the wisdom and political skill of the new sovereign. One could, however, also read it as a proclamation that not political theory and declarations but deeds and actions should be observed in the proceedings of the play and such an observation would not necessarily lead to a positive

---

[392] Hammond, Paul. 1986. "The Argument of *Measure for Measure*." In: The Massachusetts Center for Renaissance Studies. *English Literary Renaissance*. Oxford: Blackwell, Vol. 16. pp. 496-519.; pp. 512

[393] Tebbetts, Terrell L. 1985. "Talking Back to the King: *Measure for Measure* and the *Basilikon Doron*." In: West Chester State College Special Funds Office. *College Literature*. West Chester, Pa.: West Chester Univ. Press, Vol. 12. pp. 122-134.; pp. 122

[394] see Howard, Herbert. 1965. "Shakespeare's Flattery in *Measure for Measure*." In: Shakespeare Association of America. *Shakespeare Quarterly*. Washington D.C.: Folger Shakespeare Library, Vol. 16. pp. 29-37.; pp. 29

conclusion. In the Duke's ways of power we can once more observe the discrepancy between good intentions and actual rule.

The *Basilikon Doron,* however, as a main subject of public debate during the time the play was written, becomes important in other respects as well, as it proclaims caution and careful supervision of administration and advisors[395,] the strict upholding of law, especially after accession, to establish the holy order,[396] the virtue of continence[397] and the duty of a divine ruler to seek a balance between justice and mercy.[398]

The proceedings of the royal Chancery and the law courts would present the pattern for the justice and mercy motive that *Measure for Measure* elaborates more than any of its forerunners. The figure of Escalus serves as a kind of 'Master of Chancery', a *representative of the concept that on occasion conditions require relief from the letter of the law*[399]*,* attempting to soften Angelo's Puritan strictness.

We must not make a scarecrow of the law, / Setting it up to fear the birds of prey [...] Let us be keen, and rather cut a little, / Than fall, and bruise to death. (II, 1, 1-6)

Also the Duke's espionage and disguise fit in this context:

The Duke is very strangely gone from hence [...] but we do learn, / By those that know the very nerves of state, / His giving out were of an infinite distance / From his true-meant design [...] (I, 4, 50-54)

And so does the reinforcement of the fornication law and Angelo's downfall. A *play to please the king might touch a man's war against the flesh*[400], for it can be assumed that James' conviction of pre-

---

[395] *"Delite to haunt your Session and spie carefully on their proceedings."* Basilikon Doron as quoted in: Howard, Herbert; *Shakespeare's Flattery in* Measure for Measure.; pp. 29

[396] *"giving the law full execution against all breakers thereof."* Basilikon Doron as quoted in: Howard, Herbert; *Shakespeare's Flattery in* Measure for Measure.; pp. 29

[397] *"[...] fornication amongst other grievous sinnes."* Basilikon Doron as quoted in: Howard, Herbert; *Shakespeare's Flattery in* Measure for Measure.; pp. 30

[398] *"Learne also wisely to discerne betwixt Iustice and equity"* Basilikon Doron as quoted in: Dunkel, Wilbur. 1962. "Law and Equity in *Measure for Measure.*" In: Shakespeare Association of America. *Shakespeare Quarterly.* Washington D.C.: Folger Shakespeare Library, Vol. 13. pp. 275-285.; pp. 276

[399] Dunkel, Wilbur; *Law and Equity in* Measure for Measure.; pp. 282

[400] *Basilikon Doron* as quoted in: Howard, Herbert; *Shakespeare's Flattery in* Measure for Measure.; pp. 30

marriage chastity and temperance were already known in London too. Thus Angelo falls because of his immoral lust for Isabella, not for his 'execution' of Claudio, which was perhaps unnecessarily strict but legal after all.

> *He who the sword of heaven will bear / Should be as holy as severe: Pattern in himself to know, Grace to stand, and virtue, go [...] Twice treble shame on Angelo, / To weed my vice, and let his grow!* (III, 2, 254-62)

The strict enforcement of law after his accession would naturally serve a new king as a weapon against rebellion of the kind that ensued after the nine days of Queen Jane. Stability and security of succession again become important in this context and would serve as justification for a more severe persecution of opposition. The monarchy as battlement against social breakdown was firmly fixed in the Elizabethan world picture, yet there was the *fear that social chaos would honestly ensue with the exchange of James for Elisabeth*[401] among the people and the fear of rebellion among the court.

James would thus have had the right to use every measure to install his new regime, yet as the *Basilikon Doron* also tells us, once the new reign is acknowledged and accepted, means of persecution and espionage must be lowered.[402] Pursuing this kind of state control would otherwise lead to the kind of tyranny staged in *Macbeth*. His political treatise nevertheless states firmly that Christian mercy is to be evoked by a divine ruler in times of security and peace. Yet, when is a kingdom like the desired Great Britain ever to be considered wholly peaceful?

It is remarkable in that context that the Duke, although doubting Angelo's qualifications[403] decides to let him reinforce the laws of Vienna and absents himself from his realm at the brink of war. It seems that Vincentio too must undergo a careful edification to find or rediscover the divine balance of mercy and justice.[404]

---

[401] Rutledge, Douglas F. 1988. "The Structural Parallel Between Rituals of Reversal, Jacobean Political Theory, and *Measure for Measure*." In: Iowa State University of Science and Technology. *Iowa State Journal of Research*. Ames, Iowa: Iowa State Univ. Press; Vol. 62. pp. 421-441.; pp. 422

[402] see Rutledge, Douglas F. 1988. "The Structural Parallel Between Rituals of Reversal, Jacobean Political Theory, and *Measure for Measure*."; pp. 422

[403] *There is a kind of character in thy life / That to th'observer doth thy history / Fully unfold [...]* (I, 1, 26-29)

The conviction that the ways of power of a divine ruler should not be questioned by his subjects, becomes important at this point, for Vincentio lets his deputy *safe himself from the slanderous title of tyrant*[405], in letting a 'scapegoat' become the centre of disapproval, rather then himself.[406] Only the Duke's assumed purpose of educating the people of his court seems to explain his hesitancy to intervene directly, once is has become apparent that the person he has left in charge is going to go wrong.[407] He has to make his deputy repent and confess of his own free will, for he has given Angelo absolute power and the freedom to use it.[408]

James himself stated in his political discourse that only God has the right to judge a divine ruler, this verdict must therefore apply, even if the sovereign is only a surrogate for the rightful king.[409] Yet his failure and laps into tyranny would seem understandable in this context, for as a deputy he is naturally not blessed with the assumed holy wisdom of kings.[410]

James was, as had already been mentioned, keen on stylising himself as a new kind of intellectual ruler, learned and skilled in science, logic and art and divine guardian of his subjects.

> *A gentleman of all temperance [...] He professes to have received no sinister measure from his judge, but most willingly humbles himself to the determination of justice.*
> (III, 2, 203-210)

These Solomonic qualities of the Duke's rule in Vienna are of course counterbalanced with Angelo's tyranny – who like Macbeth falls because he sets his own desires above those of his kingdom.

> *Or whether that the body public be / A horse whereon the governor doth ride [...] He can command [...] Whether the tyranny be in his place,* (I, 2, 140-144)

---

[404] *Sith 'twas my fault to give the people scope, / 'Twould be my tyranny to strike and gall them* (I, 3, 35-36)

[405] Rutledge, Douglas F. 1988. "The Structural Parallel Between Rituals of Reversal, Jacobean Political Theory, and *Measure for Measure*."; pp. 430

[406] *Why, here's a change indeed in the commonwealth.* (I, 2, 87)

[407] *Lent him our terror, dressed him with our love,* (I, 1, 19)

[408] *And punish them to your height of pleasure.* (V, 1, 238)

[409] Rutledge, Douglas F.; *The Structural Parallel Between Rituals of Reversal, Jacobean Political Theory, and* Measure for Measure.; pp. 437

[410] *When I perceive your Grace, like power divine, / Hath looked upon my passes.* (V, 1, 362-63)

But not only Angelo lacks the divine insight of temperance and virtue, Isabella is also tested and tried - reminiscent of *The Merchant of Venice* – to impose on her the *Christian duty of self-sacrifice.*[411] The changing imagery under James after Elisabeth's long and predominantly successful rule naturally included changing attitudes for example towards femininity and marriage, already observed in *Macbeth*. Thus the Duke's sudden proposal to marry Isabella becomes less surprising in the context of the *Basilikon Doron* than it would be in a modern society. Her obvious virtues of mercy, moral strength, eloquence and overall obedience make her almost a blueprint for the kind of woman *a prince should marry and as to the propriety of the unromantic approach toward matrimony which a ruler should take.*[412]

The friars disguise in this context alludes to the combination of monarchical and clerical authority[413] and also underlines chastity and abstinence Vincentio seeks in order to find divine edification. Still it remains questionable if these strands of the *Basilikon Doron* were really embedded in the play to flatter King James, or if they in contrast hide some points of criticism. The conviction of divine rule is stressed here as it will be in *Macbeth*, but as with Macbeth too, the rightful ruler still has to counterbalance the tendency to use such power arbitrarily.[414]

The main assumption among critics for a long time was nevertheless that not only must the Duke be associated with King James, but this association should also be a positive one. [415] Certainly the fact that the figure of the Duke was inserted into the material taken from Whetstone and given such a centre position would hint at the specific importance of Vincentio and his political discourse in a *first flush at*

---

[411] *Basilikon Doron* as quoted in: Howard, Herbert; *Shakespeare's Flattery in* Measure for Measure.; pp. 32

[412] Stevenson, David L. 1959. "The Role of James I. in Shakespeare's *Measure for Measure.*" In: Allen, Don Cameron (ed.). *English Literary History* Baltimore, Maryland: Johns Hopkins Univ. Press, Vol. 26. pp. 188-209.; pp. 196

[413] Dunkel, Wilbur; *Law and Equity in* Measure for Measure.; pp. 280

[414] *Thus can the demi-God, Authority, / Make us pay down for our offence [...] The words of heaven; on whom it will, it will, / On whom it will not, so; yet still 'tis just.* (I, 2, 102-105)

[415] *Let him be but testimonied in his own bringings-forth, and he shall appear to the envious a scholar, a statesman, a soldier.* (III, 2, 123-125)

the post-Elizabethan era.[416] His similarity to James becomes obvious when his refusal to stage himself to his subjects mirrors the king's sentiments[417] and his consoling of Claudio takes the tone of a fatalistic melancholy.[418]
Yet as has already been hinted in the first lines of the play, some of the Duke's de facto actions bring *some of James's assumptions into real question.*[419] The *Basilikon Doron* admits some early flaws in James' rule, as far as the strict handling of justice is concerned that he wants his son to avoid. A divine ruler has in all respects to be a virtuous example to his people: *And above all, let the measure of your love to every one, be according to the measure of his virtue.*[420]
Slanders against this kind of holy rule can only be uttered out of ignorance and must therefore be silenced and punished. The slanders voiced by Lucio and his punishment exemplify this conviction, but it is to question if his rude remarks really serve only as a comic interlude for the Jacobean courtiers, who lived with intrigues and whispers every day. The image of the somewhat hypocritical Duke he develops reminds us far more of King James as he would presumably have liked. *While James touted his virtue, moderation, and piety, the reality of his life and rule was anything but praiseworthy.*[421] Lucio in his function as comical villain shows us James' love of excessive feasts,[422] his bisexuality[423] and his

---

[416] Stevenson, David ; *The Role of James I. in Shakespeare's* Measure for Measure.; pp. 189

[417] *I'll privily away. I love the people, / But I do not like to stage me to their eyes:* (I, 1, 67-68)

[418] *Reason thus with life: / If I do lose thee, I do lose a thing / That none but fools would keep [...]* (III, 1, 6-8)

[419] Tebbetts, Terrell ; *Talking Back to the King*: Measure for Measure *and the* Basilikon Doron.; pp. 123

[420] *Basilikon Doron* as quoted in: Stevenson, David ; *The Role of James I. in Shakespeare's* Measure for Measure.; pp. 201

[421] Brown, Carolyn E. 1996. "Duke Vincentio of *Measure for Measure* and *King James I.* of England: The Poorest Princes in Christendom." In: Clio; Clio-Institute University of Wisconsin, Bloomington: Indiana Univ. Press, Vol. 26, pp. 51-78.; pp. 52

[422] *He would be drunk too, that let me inform you.* (III, 2, 112)

[423] *He had some felling for the sport; he knew the service; and that instructed him to mercy. – I have never heard the absent Duke much detected for women; he was not inclined that way.* (III, 2, 104-107)

depressive moods and unwillingness to mingle with his common subjects.[424] This bad reputation of James' was common knowledge even before his accession, and he was frequently satirised as *the wisest fool in Christendom.*[425]
Still Lucio, in some way, defends his flawed ruler and makes him much more likeable in a way than the virtuous manner adopted by the Duke himself.[426] Especially Lucio's punishment of imprisonment and marriage with a whore, which in the end comes under the heading of 'mercy', as he is not to be executed, gives a certain irony to the Duke's holy wisdom.[427] It his been proposed that this sequence is more probably included to stress Vincentio's similarity to King James, who was said to be very indignant when confronted with criticism.[428]
The conviction that a divine ruler, perfected by learning and wisdom, is not the be criticised, yet satirized by his subjects is of course embedded in James' political worldview, yet in Shakespeare this infallibility of a monarch is frequently contradicted, as can be see in Macbeth, Lear, Claudius or even Hamlet.[429]
So we come back to the contrast of ideology and actual deed, which would make *Measure for Measure* not a flattery but a political satire instead.[430] The change in the literary sources and the centre position of the Duke would thus lead to the proposal that the convictions and plans appraised by King James in the *Basilikon Doron* were regrettably not permuted into actual policy. The Duke himself, however, remains convinced of his infallibility – and so perhaps would have been King James, which would have made *Measure for*

---

[424] *A shy fellow was the Duke; and I believe I know the cause of his withdrawing [...] A very superficial, ignorant, unweighing fellow.* (III, 2, 114-121)
[425] Brown, Carolyn E.; *Duke Vincentio of* Measure for Measure *and King James I. of England:*; pp. 53
[426] *[...] if the old fantastical Duke of dark corners had been at home, he had lived.* (IV, 3, 147-48)
[427] Dunkel, Wilbur; *Law and Equity in* Measure for Measure.; pp. 278
[428] *Marrying a punk, my lord, is pressing to death, / Whipping, and hanging. – Slandering a prince deserves it.* (V, 1, 514-16)
[429] *[...] The state whereon I studied / Is, like a good thing being often read, / Grown sere and tedious [...]* (II, 4, 7-9)
[430] Tebbetts, Terrell ; *Talking Back to the King*: Measure for Measure *and the* Basilikon Doron.; pp. 124

Measure 'safe' for court performance, assuming that the King would see it as a confirmation of his policy.[431]
The friars disguise in this context becomes a satirical edge too, as far as the monarch's fatherly concern for his subjects is concerned. The clerical authority assumed by Vincentio would present him with no actual power in England, but with a halo of mercy and virtue that is needed to manipulate the course of action. In a clerical role the Duke assumes the god-like mastery over life and death[432] that the divine ruler is attributed in King James' *True Law*.[433]
He thus bents Angelo's and Isabella's lives to his purpose, but the 'greater good' for which these sacrifices are made remains unseen. As it is, Angelo is revealed as the hypocrite and tyrant he has become under the Duke's burden, to stress Vincentio's own mystique and power. He ignores his plea to be tested in politics first[434] and watches him fall as easily as he ignores Isabella's wish for silence and chastity, plays with her emotions and seizes her himself.[435] Thus if Angelo is a hypocrite *the Duke's early actions show that he is one too*.[436]
In Vincentio's treatment of Angelo, however, we can also find signs of James' much criticised practises of favouritism, ignorant of skill or moral strength of the favoured[437] and often promoting them far beyond more suitable candidates. The Duke of *Measure for Measure* demonstrated that in his treatment of Angelo and Escalus:

> *In our remove be thou at full ourself. / Mortality and mercy in Vienna [...] Old Escalus, / Though first in question, is thy secondary.* (I, 1, 43-46)

---

[431] see Tebbetts, Terrell ; *Talking Back to the King*: Measure for Measure *and the* Basilikon Doron.; pp. 126
[432] *It was a mad, fantastical trick of him to steal from the state and usurp the beggary he was never born to.* (III, 2, 82-83)
[433] see Stevenson, David ; *The Role of James I. in Shakespeare's* Measure for Measure.; pp. 205
[434] *Let there be some more test made of my metal* (I, 1, 48)
[435] *But I will keep her ignorant of her good, / To make her heavenly comforts of despair / When it is least expected.* (IV, 3, 100-102)
[436] Tebbetts, Terrell ; *Talking Back to the King*: Measure for Measure *and the* Basilikon Doron.; pp. 129
[437] *A blasting and a scandalous breath to fall / On him so near us? [...]* (V, 1, 122-23)

In addition to that Vincentio never lets official blame fall on Angelo, even after he himself knows of his inadequacy in a moral[438] as well as in a judicial sense.[439] King James' personal favourite during this time, the Earl of Arran, was said to be vain and also cruel, but was equally favoured by his king, who was *more concerned with pleasing his favourite than with protecting his subjects.*[440] This flaw in James' character had even been discovered by Queen Elisabeth, who had reprimanded him in definite words:

> *[...] I smile to see 'how childish, foolish and witless' a tool you were in the hands of these three traitor lords [...] For your own sake play the King and let your subjects see you respect yourself.*[441]

A passage in fewer words echoed by Isabella:

[...] but oh, how much is the good Duke deceived in Angelo![442]

In the end Vincentio rids himself of his former favourite in a public event, very unlike his 'former' self.[443]
Vincentio thus charges him with questionable arguments and destroys his political career. Consequently the position of Vincentio as the fatherly monarch of his realm crumbles in the last act, when both law and the sanctuary of marriage suffer from his interference, as shall be shown in the next chapter. If the play, however, was intended as a criticism of James' rule, it would have undertaken the dangerous attempt to put the audience in a quasi 'god-like' position, from which to judge the infallible monarch. Thus *Measure for Measure* would *somehow reduce the king to a position low enough to be judged.*[444]

---

[438] *[...] Angelo had never the purpose to corrupt her;* (III, 1, 160-61)

[439] *It is a bitter deputy. – Not so, not so; his life is paralleled / Even with the stroke and line of his great justice:* (IV, 2, 65-67)

[440] Brown, Carolyn E.; *Duke Vincentio of* Measure for Measure *and King James I. of England:*; pp. 60

[441] Brown, Carolyn E.; *Duke Vincentio of* Measure for Measure *and King James I. of England:*; pp. 61

[442] III, 1, 186-87

[443] *The Duke yet would have dark deeds darkly answered, he would never bring them to light.* (III, 2, 150-52)

[444] Rutledge, Douglas F.; *The Structural Parallel Between Rituals of Reversal, Jacobean Political Theory, and* Measure for Measure.; pp. 439

Isabella, the Duke and the Trial Scene

> *Rather, speechlessness can also be interpreted as a refusal to ascent positively to the control of an "other". It is for this reason [...] that Isabella's silence reverberates in our minds long after the play is done.*[445]

To understand the figure of the Duke and to evaluate his actions, the last act of the trial scene and his interaction with the other characters is most important. His treatment of Angelo has been elaborated in the last chapter; this now will focus on two other persons essential for the Duke's 'dealing out' of mercy – Isabella and Lucio.

The justice and mercy motive observed in *Measure for Measure* becomes, as has been shown before, already apparent in its unusual title. Other than most Shakespeare plays it has at first no visible connection to its plot, but the biblical allusion, the law of the old Testament 'an eye for an eye' is evoked in the trial scene, as is the Christian virtue of mercy expressed in the New Testament. On Isabella's first appearance she is willing to submit herself under the strict rules of a Catholic nunnery, accepting her seclusion from the outward world and her vow of silence.[446]

This religious motive is somewhat continued in her encounter with Angelo, where he is conducting the part of the tempting devil, contorting the meaning of sin and virtue[447] while Isabella enacts the part of the pure virgin, who sees directly through his vain pretence.[448]

---

[445] Lechter-Siegel, Amy. 1992. "Isabella's Silence: The Consolidation of Power in Measure for Measure." In: Di Cesare, Mario A. (ed.). *Reconsidering the Renaissance.* Binghamton, N.Y.: Medieval and Renaissance Texts and Studies Press; Vol. 33. pp. 371-80.; pp. 380

[446] *Then, if you must not show your face; / Or if you show your face, you must not speak,* (I, 4, 12-13)

[447] *Might there not be a charity in sin / To save this brother's life?* (II, 4, 61-63)

[448] *Plainly conceive, I love you. – My brother did love Juliet, / And you tell me that he shall die for 't.* (II, 4, 142-44)

Isabella's arguments become more and more ethically superior[449] to Angelo's strict and partial construction of the letter of law, showing the *discrepancy between divine law and human capacity.*[450]
The play presents in these scenes a strange likeness between Isabella and Portia in their strong eloquence, but while Portia has her disguise in which she can act out her equity freely, Isabella has to plead demurely with Angelo and to try to make him see the consequence of his strict measuring:

> *If he had been as you, and you as he, / You would have slipp'd like him, but he like you / Would not have been so stern.* (II, 2, 64-66)

It is remarkable, however, that both Angelo and Isabella try to 'depersonalise' the mechanism justice to refrain from being held responsible for offence[451] and also law.[452] As they are not, as is the Duke, blessed with a divine sense of justice, this again could appeal to the holy mission of King James.

In the end the measure of mercy in Isabella triumphs over the measure of revenge. A plot like this could have been taken from an old morality tale, ending in Angelo's atonement and Isabella's admission to her desired convent. That this does not happen is only due to the Duke's decision and feminist criticism sees the reason for it in Isabella's threat for the renaissance society and a personification of the old feud between crown and church.[453] As a virgin and a novice, it is argued, Isabella puts herself outside both the personal and the worldly authority of Vincentio. His tutelage as a friar would thus not develop Isabella's character, but somewhat diminish her independent standing.

James' position as a divine ruler was based on three major assumptions of him as *a good Christian, a good ruler, [and] good social and moral being.*[454] The lining up is important in this context, as renaissance thought still proclaimed the supremacy of God over

---

[449] *[...] lawful mercy / Is nothing kin to foul redemption.* (II, 4, 112-13)
[450] Hammond, Paul; *The Argument of* Measure for Measure.; pp. 501
[451] *I do beseech you, let it be his fault, / And not my brother.* (II, 2, 35-36)
[452] *It is the law, not I, condemn your brother;* (II, 2, 80)
[453] Lechter-Siegel, Amy; *Isabella's Silence: The Consolidation of Power in* Measure for Measure.; pp. 372
[454] Lechter-Siegel, Amy; *Isabella's Silence: The Consolidation of Power in* Measure for Measure.; pp. 373

any worldly rule. King Henry had overturned the power of the clergy, but still in James' times religion was seen as a potential danger for the divine monarch, as seen in his encounters with Catholic or Presbyterian parties. Thus Vincentio's friars habit does not only underline his twofold authority, but he also voices exactly the sort of clerical resistance that would be most feared by James:
[...] the Duke / Dare no more stretch this finger of mine than he / Dare rack his own. His subject am I not.[455]
Concerning Isabella, however, it must be clearly stated that her ability of resistance would be negligible, for as a nun she would have to submit to him, as she must as a wife. *The Duke's use of marriage is an absolutist strategy which can be at variance with individual desire.*[456] Here again all meaning lies in the interpretation of Isabella's silence. It alone can make Vincentio – and James – absolute tyrant or divine ruler, even if by no means he will probably become the romantic hero.
Finally, in the trial scene the motives of Christian mercy and legal law are once more confronted. This kind of Christian theology was not only a question of faith in renaissance England, but also of realpolitik as every individual to hold power was supposed to *think how Christ would judge, before they judge.*[457]
Only God would have the power to oversee all things with equal measure and he could impart this kind of knowledge – theoretically – into his worldly lieutenant.[458]
Such intermingling of political and theological arguments became a central part of renaissance education and the arguments between Angelo and Escalus, Angelo and Isabella or even, to a satirical extent, Pompey and Froth, exemplify this rhetoric elaboration of statecraft and law:[459]

---

[455] V, 1, 309-11
[456] Lechter-Siegel, Amy; *Isabella's Silence: The Consolidation of Power in* Measure for Measure.; pp. 379
[457] Siegel, pp. N. 1953. "*Measure for Measure*: The Significance of the Title." In: Shakespeare Association of America. *Shakespeare Quarterly*. Washington D.C.: Folger Shakespeare Library, Vol. 4. pp.317-321.; pp. 317
[458] *[...] O, it is excellent / To have a giant's strength, but it is tyrannous / To use it like a giant.* (II, 2, 108-10)
[459] see Hammond, Paul; *The Argument of* Measure for Measure.; pp. 499

> *The law hath not been dead, though it hath slept: / Those many had not dared to do that evil / If the first that did th'edict infringe / Had answered for this deed.* (II, 2, 91-94)

A rightful ruler on the other hand had to combine these two concepts of Christian mercy and legal justice, as he had the combine his divine and common 'body'. Again the Duke disguised as friar mirrors this combination of authorities that can not be hidden by mere clothing.[460] The fatherly aspect also becomes important in the before mentioned healing powers of the monarch, quite bodily in the case of the King's Evil, but moreover in a sense of body politic. Thus *King James looked upon the opening of the new reign as an opportunity to tighten up laws which had fallen into disuse*[461], to present himself to his new subjects as keeper of the peace and holy order:

> *I show it most of all when I show justice; / For then I pity those I do not know, / Which a dismissed offence would after gall,* (II, 2, 103-105)

Yet many of his new decrees were not enforced in the rural parts of the country, or executed with a heedless rigor,[462] forcing the king to opt severely for a greater control of state measures to prevent the abuse of power on which *Measure for Measure* reflects.[463]

But *Measure for Measure* includes not only King James convictions about monarchy, but also some judicial statements, for example *his insistence that prisoners either be punished or pardoned*[464], instead of having them locked away in the tower:

> *How came it that the absent Duke had not either delivered him to his liberty, or executed him? I have heard it was ever his manner to do so.* (IV, 2, 115-17)

In one case, however, this conviction of persecution or pardon left James and this was in addition a public topic of some controversy during the time *Measure for Measure* was written.[465]

---

[460] *[...] Grace is grace, despite all controversy:* (I, 2, 21)
[461] Hammond, Paul; *The Argument of* Measure for Measure.; pp. 514
[462] *Because authority, though it err like others [...] ask your heart what it doth know / That's like my brother's fault.* (II, 2, 135-39)
[463] see Hammond, Paul; *The Argument of* Measure for Measure.; pp. 516
[464] Wasson, John. 1970. "*Measure for Measure*: A Text for Court Performance?." In: Shakespeare Association of America. *Shakespeare Quarterly*. Washington D.C.: Folger Shakespeare Library, Vol. 21. pp. 17-24.; pp. 17
[465] *'Tis one thing to be tempted, Escalus, / Another thing to fall.* (II, 1, 17-18)

Shortly after King James had reached London, some English noblemen were arrested for plotting and resistance against the new regime, cases which became known as the *Main- and Bye Plots*.[466] Although these 'conspiracies' were not much more then public slandering and had no consequences in a historical sense, they are valuable for the understanding of *Measure for Measure*, because they exemplify the acute staging of justice undertaken, not by Vincentio, but King James.

In the course of the investigations several of Elisabeth's old courtiers were imprisoned, including the Lords Grey and Cobham, and Elisabeth's old favourite Lord Raleigh, who was convicted on the sole evidence of Cobham's confession. Raleigh had profited shortly from Essex downfall, but was not very popular among the people of London. In the play he is most probably found in the figure of Lucio, which whom he shares the ‚fantastic' character and the fondness of slandering his king. Raleigh himself had made some derisive comments about the new king's inability to distinguish between friend and foe – probably aimed at the 'uncivilized' and 'brutish', as it seemed to English eyes, Scottish favourites.[467]

James' was known to persecute such slanders rigorously, but when he, eager to convict Raleigh, *stepped into the picture as actor, director and playwright*[468] the bravado and dignity of Raleigh's defence turned the public opinion favourably. Still all three Lords were sentenced to death.

King James albeit had secretly decided to pardon them[469], but kept his messenger from relaying the news until each man had ascended the scaffold.[470] The exact wording of the pardon was probably written by James himself and drew considerable jubilations from the

---

[466] Bernthal, Craig A. 1992. "Staging Justice: James I. and the Trial Scenes of *Measure for Measure*." In: Patten, Robert L.(ed.). *Studies in English Literature 1500-1900*. Houston, Texas: Johns Hopkins University Press. Vol. 32. pp. 247-269.; pp. 248

[467] Brown, Carolyn E.; *Duke Vincentio of* Measure for Measure *and King James I. of England*: pp. 64

[468] Bernthal, Craig A.; *Staging Justice: James I. and the Trial Scenes of* Measure for Measure.; pp. 250

[469] *[...] I have seen / When, after execution, judgement hath / Repented o'er his doom.* (II, 2, 10-12)

[470] Bernthal, Craig A.; *Staging Justice: James I. and the Trial Scenes of* Measure for Measure.; pp. 252

assembled crowd. Still Raleigh and his fellow prisoners returned to the tower and were kept there, in Raleigh's case for over a decade. Public feeling about this kind of 'mercy' is also expressed in the play:
> There is a devilish mercy in the judge, / If you'll implore it, that will free your life, / But fetter you till death. (III, 1, 64-66)

Shakespeare's trial scene embeds much of these confused events in Vincentio's pretence of support for Angelo, his reappearance as a friar, his sudden all-concluding decisions. In his course of argument he forces Isabella to become a symbol of mercy, while he condemns Angelo to become the vice figure, as he himself is stylised as master of justice and equity – *political theatre is used to create state power*.[471]

The charge and pardon of Claudio seem doubtful in this context, merely a mechanism to form Isabella and in the trial scene it becomes equally doubtful that *Angelo is legally [...] guilty of anything*.[472] After all his charge on Claudio was hypocritical, but not false and his intent on raping Isabella was never acted out. A bad intent however was not punishable by renaissance law, as Isabella points out:
> [...] My brother had but justice, / In that he did for what he died. / For Angelo, / His act did not o'ertake his bad intent, / And must be buried but as an intent (V, 1, 441-45)

His fornication with Mariana thus remains his only offence, brought about by non other than Vincentio himself. The disputable evidence and the questionable punishment are motives found in the Raleigh trial, as is Barnadine's refusal to accept his death sentence.[473]

King James' official reasoning for pardoning Raleigh was his unwillingness to confess his guilt[474] – which after all presented an essential part of renaissance justice.[475] The unrepentant murderer Barnadine is yet somewhat punished equal to his crime by obtaining

---

[471] Bernthal, Craig A.; *Staging Justice: James I. and the Trial Scenes of* Measure for Measure.; pp. 256

[472] Bernthal, Craig A.; *Staging Justice: James I. and the Trial Scenes of* Measure for Measure.; pp. 258

[473] *I swear I will not die today for any man's persuasion.* (IV, 3, 51)

[474] *A creature unprepared, unmeet for death [...] whiles I / Persuade this rude wretch willingly to die.* (IV, 3, 58-72)

[475] see Bernthal, Craig A.; *Staging Justice: James I. and the Trial Scenes of* Measure for Measure.; pp. 263

his freedom in this world, while being instructed about his awaiting eternal punishment in the next – an example how 'mercy' can even be crueller than retribution, reminiscent of Shylock, and also clearly visible in Lucio's fate of imprisonment and dishonour. *James's inhumanity toward Ralegh, in particular, is reflected in the Duke's treatment of Lucio.*[476]
Raleigh himself was kept 13 years in the tower to be still executed in 1618. Yet this development could not have been considered by Shakespeare but adds a kind of historical irony to the one shown in the play.
The solution of the trial scene and the contrast between the Duke's mercy and Angelo's strictness of justice thus presents *the basis for recognizing the necessity for justice with equity.*[477] Yet the Duke's endeavour to restore law and order in Vienna seems flawed in action, if not in intent. He has set out to enforce stricter rules and in the end pardons everyone, even Lucio and, in a way, Barnadine. His attempt on prohibiting fornication meanwhile seems equally questionable in the light of three forced marriages.[478]
Vincentio's final announcement that he will explain how all this came to pass in his palace leaves the reader somewhat confused, for he is excluded from the decisions and explanations, similar to the parties involved in the Bye-Plot *for whom the king staged a public execution, one which he secretly did not intend to enact.*[479] Thus to find the balance between mercy and justice remains a royal domain and prerogative, and *Measure for Measure* tries to reflect how this kind of royal balance is sought, disturbed and found by different means, while is *a little reluctantly, takes apart the [...] equity and reciprocity epitomized in its own title.*[480]
It is assumed that the Folio text of *Measure for Measure* includes the actual performance that was given in Whitehall due to the almost complete absence of stage directions, settings and scenery, which would suggest an adaptation for a setting like a banquet hall rather

---

[476] Brown, Carolyn E.; *Duke Vincentio of* Measure for Measure *and King James I. of England:*; pp. 72

[477] Dunkel, Wilbur; *Law and Equity in* Measure for Measure.; pp. 285

[478] *Some rise by sin, and some by virtue fall.* (II, 1, 38)

[479] Brown, Carolyn E.; *Duke Vincentio of* Measure for Measure *and King James I. of England:*; pp. 53

[480] Hammond, Paul; *The Argument of* Measure for Measure.; pp. 519

then a furnished professional theatre.[481] We could thus suspect that some passages of character silence – like Isabella's – could be interpreted quite differently before the king than they would be on London's stages, varying the flattery and critique in equal measure. *Thus theatre enters the blood of the sovereign, through that, the body politic, and through that once again, the theatres.*[482]

---
[481] Wasson, John; Measure for Measure: *A Text for Court Performance?*.; pp. 22
[482] Bernthal, Craig A.; *Staging Justice: James I. and the Trial Scenes of* Measure for Measure.; pp. 265

The Winter's Tale

> Love, miracle, gift, resurrection, forgiveness [...] themes that have dominated the critical and performance afterlife of The Winter's Tale, a late play and one of Shakespeare's most theatrically self-conscious and emotionally exhausting.[483]

The Winter's Tale as one of Shakespeare's last works and is often considered to be an example for his artistic accomplishment, along with The Tempest, with which it shares the fairy tale atmosphere and uncertain tone, either fit for a *tragedy, ironic comedy, or fantasy*.[484] Like *Measure for Measure* it was soon discarded by the Restauration age, because it lacked the aristotelian concept and clearness of message that became the fashion of the later 17th century.[485] And again, as its forerunner, it was rediscovered as a play for potentially radical reproductions by the following centuries. The Victorian Age in particular saw a great number of 'Winter Tales'[486], often richly furnished with the splendour of antiquity, presumably boarding on the fashionable archaeology interests of the time.

Like almost all of Shakespeare's later plays it is accounted for as 'problematic' because of the before mentioned uncertainty of tone and purpose, the difficulty of production and the ambiguous character motivation and outline. Experimental reconcilliation[487] is a term that could be used to describe the plays purpose and context. The experimental nature of the text – combining fairy tale motives, pastoral idylls and structures of monarchy – mostly relies on the deliberate artificialness of its atmosphere and context and the embedded but also meta-level conflict of art relating the nature of

---

[483] Snyder, Susan. 2007. "Introduction." In: Snyder, Susan (ed.). *Shakespeare, William; The Winter's Tale; New Cambridge Shakespeare Ed.* Cambridge: Cambridge Univ. Press.; pp. 1

[484] Grene, David. 1967. *Reality and the Heroic Pattern. Last Plays of Ibsen, Shakespeare, and Sophocles.* London: Univ. of Chicago Press. pp. 68-86.; pp. 68

[485] Geisen, Herbert. 2000. „Nachwort." In: Geisen, Herbert (ed.). *Shakespeare, William; The Winter's Tale; Zweisprachige Ausgabe.* Stuttgart: Reclam.; pp. 231

[486] see Geisen, Herbert. 2000. „Nachwort." ;pp. 232

[487] Geisen, Herbert; *Nachwort*; pp. 233

human behaviour. The play itself recalls the contexts of *King Lear* and shows – as shall be discussed later – some aspects of Shakespeare's last history play *King Henry VIII.* Shakespeare also profited from romance tales, which were part of the English tradition since the early medieval *Canterbury Tales*[488] and again includes strands from religious miracle and morality plays.

Date and Source
The Winter's Tale is frequently placed in the chronology of Shakespeare's works after *Pericles* and *Cymbeline* but before *The Tempest.*[489] The allusions to the satyrs in the pastoral scene[490] are assumed to relate to *Jonson's* Masque of Oberon *performed for King James on 1 January 1611.*[491] However, the exact time of the composition is highly questioned among critics and dated back even to 1609, before *Cymbeline*. Arguments are issued for all of those datings naturally, but neither can be assumed final.[492] It is almost certain, however, that the play was performed at court in November 1611[493], which would support to the conclusion that it was written not long before, as the plays performed at court were most probably picked for their timely popularity.

Shakespeare leaned on a pastoral play issued by Robert Greene in 1588, which had been reprinted several times and lastly in 1607.[494] *Pandosto, The Triumph of Time* already included most of the basic plot-line of *The Winter's Tale* and most of its major characters too, although some quite important changes were made, which could be of interest for a historical analysis. For one thing, the reversal of places is noticeable in Shakespeare's adaptation, for Pandosto rules Bohemia, while his counterpart is King of Sicilia. Sicilia presents, however, a far more interesting setting for the beginning and end of the action, for it contains the fabled realm of Arcadia *but also the*

---
[488] Geisen, Herbert; *Nachwort*; pp. 235
[489] see Snyder, Susan; *Introduction*; pp. 62
[490] *They call themselves saltiers and they have a dance [...]* (IV, 4, 308) All quotes from the primary text are taken from: Shakespeare, William. 2007. *The Winter's Tale*. Cambridge: Cambridge Univ. Press.
[491] Snyder, Susan; *Introduction*; pp. 62
[492] see Snyder, Susan; *Introduction*; pp. 63
[493] Steele, Mary Susan; *Plays & Masques at Court During the Reigns of Elisabeth, James and Charles.*; pp. 168
[494] see Snyder, Susan; *Introduction*; pp. 66

'mythological county of classical literature' that was home to monsters, giants, tyrannous kings and malignant gods.[495]
The realm of Bohemia, associated with rural idyll and peace, would serve much better for the pastoral that Greene centred on, and Shakespeare preserved there, but Sicilia presents a more fitting kingdom for a king like Leontes.[496]
Greene's play is thus altogether not a fairy tale and King Pandosto, for example, has much more time to find evidence and dwell on the subject of his wife's betrayal, than Leontes is given by Shakespeare. In addition to that, Greene introduces, via his counsellor Franion, reasoned argument and political considerations to his play, while Shakespeare reduces his Camillo to shock and indignation, when confronted with the king's doubts:

My wife's a hobby-horse [...] 'Shrew my heart, / You never spoke what did become you less / Than this, which to reiterate were sin / As deep as that, though true. (I, 2, l. 273-81)

A kind of argumentative advice, though in a much different tone, is given by Paulina instead[497] a figure of Shakespeare's own invention to counterbalance the demure and stoical women figures of Hermione and Perdita, which will be considered in the next chapters. Shakespeare also changed the 'role' of Time in his play, which in Greene's original had much more of a deliberate nature, rather then the omniscient, wise fate-like part Shakespeare gives his chorus.[498]
On the other hand, Shakespeare devises a happy ending reminiscent of *Measure for Measure* with the *deus ex machina* of Hermione's resurrection, while Greene followed the more plausible line of letting his Pandosto commit suicide once the succession of his kingdom is secured, to pay for his sins against his wife.
It is widely assumed that ancient classics like Ovid's *Metamorphoses*[499] served as basis for some of Shakespeare's additions of the pastoral structure. Ovid's original tales had just been

---

[495] Snyder, Susan; *Introduction*; pp. 67

[496] *[...] you shall see, as I have said, great difference betwixt our Bohemia and your Sicilia.* (I, 1, 2-4)

[497] *I am as ignorant in that as you / In so entitling me, and no less honest / Than you are mad [...]* (II, 3, 68-71)

[498] *[...] both joy and terror / Of good and bad, that makes and unfolds error,* (IV, 1, 1-2)

[499] see Snyder, Susan; *Introduction*; pp. 70

translated and published in London in 1567 and provided for example the tale of Prosperina – the goddess of flowers and spring, often recalled as Flora – and her goddess mother Demeter, who brings frost about the land as she searches for her lost daughter. Another story features Pygmalion and his beloved statue, which turns alive at his desperate plea. There had been a classical tradition of pastorals too, but this romance tradition in antiquity had already been satirized by classic authors like Theokrit, who counterbalanced the rural idyll with the corruption and perversion of city and court. In these ancient pastorals the 'Petrarchcan' motif of wooing an inaccessible lady was foreshadowed and elegies were sung to stylise a deceased beloved into a kind of demigoddess.[500] The medieval mystery and morality plays in addition provided tales of tests and trials for a loving couple and also the godly intervention on their behalf. Strands of all these motives can be found in *Pandosto* as well, but while Greene's play stays a mere pastoral romance, Shakespeare seemed more interested in creating an elizabethan-style fairy-tale.[501]

This connection is most pronounced in the ongoing debates about the relation of art and nature, which was a topic for intellectual debate in London, as the Puritans declared all art to be pretence – especially of course the theatre – and all pretence to be lies and all lies, naturally, to be sins. Another noted literate of the English Renaissance, Sir Phillip Sidney, had published a defence of literature called *An Apologie for Poetry* already in 1595:

> *Only the poet [...] doth grow, in effect, into another nature, in making things either better than nature bringeth forth, or quite anew [...]*[502]

This defence of the poetic license could be found in Shakespeare too:

> *Yet nature is made better by no mean [...] This is an art / Which does mend nature – change it rather – but / The art itself is nature.* (IV, 4, 89-97)

Shakespeare presents in *The Winter's Tale* a sceptic development of his own earlier romances, like *As You Like It* or *Much Ado About Nothing.*[503] His lovers, Perdita and Florizel, are threatened, not by vice-figures like Autolycus, but by their own families and Perdita's

---
[500] see Geisen, Herbert; *Nachwort*; pp. 240
[501] Geisen, Herbert; *Nachwort*; pp. 237
[502] *An Apologie for Poetry* as quoted in: Geisen, Herbert; *Nachwort*; pp. 236
[503] see Geisen, Herbert; *Nachwort*; pp. 241

and Hermione's stoic resignation is counterbalanced by Paulina's successful temper. The idyll is threatened by reality and reality is denied in the fairy tale ending. The ancient and petrarchcan myths of love and virtue were subjected to a sceptical, yet realistic, examination in Shakespeare's sonnets already, but it seems that in *The Winter's Tale* this sceptic design is reflected onto the stage.

Plot and Structure
The Winter's Tale keeps the tragic-comedy aspects already observed in *Measure for Measure* and the *deus ex machina* ending that, most literally, miraculously provides an all-embracing solution. It also features the union of three couples – Leontes and Hermione, Florizel and Perdita and lastly Claudio and Paulina, whose marriage is undertaken in much the same way as Angelo's had been and passes in equal silence of the concerned characters.[504]
The last words of the play too remind of the ending of the *Merchant of Venice*, promising a peaceful and joyful life, happily ever after, for all concerned and thus provide the grounds on which all three plays are considered to be comedies. And yet the title of the play – in the play's own context – would hint at a more tragic story, as *A sad tale's best for winter [...]*.[505] Indeed the play shows some resemblance to the tragedy of *Macbeth*, when Leontes' disease and mad jealousy causes disruptions in the natural order, seen for example in the bear attack or the storm destroying Sicilian ships. Also Leontes is haunted by the insomnia that is evoked by grief and desperation. Unlike Macbeth, however, he is sent a rescuing 'angel' in the form of Paulina.[506]
In the end, however, the return of Perdita – like the return of spring – provides the cure for all those tensions and secures the peace and freedom of Sicilia and overrides the differences between the gloomy court of Leontes and the Eden-like Bohemia. Only through this happy reconciliation does the fairy tale character of the play survive, albeit tinged with realism – *real life transformed into a fairy tale or a fairy tale coming alive.*[507]

---

[504]*Come Camillo, / And take her by the hand [...]* (V, 3, 143-44)
[505]II, 1, 25
[506]*I / Do come with words as medical as true, / Honest, as either, to purge him of that humour / That presses him from sleep.* (II, 3, 35-39)

The design of ancient pastorals is kept in the idyllic atmosphere of the sheep-shearing scene, serving as a contrast to the tyranny of Leontes and the tragic deaths ruling the first half of the play. Nevertheless, the pastoral romance is rudely disturbed by Polixenes, who turns out to be but a *paler*[508] personification of Leontes, bringing something of the same injustice Perdita received in Sicilia upon his own court and throwing threats at his own son and successor.[509] The differences between Sicilia and Bohemia thus get smaller and only by the miracle solution of the last act a catastrophe for both royal houses is avoided.

It must be noted, however, that one of the politically most important themes of the play, namely the question of succession, is not really answered by Perdita's return. In the early phase of Leontes' jealousy, the possibility of a queen's infidelity presents itself as the main threat to succession in a patriarchal society.[510] Leontes wants Perdita to be abandoned for he will not have a descendant of Polixenes near his throne.[511] It is almost ironical therefore that in the end Perdita – although suddenly heir to Leontes due to the surprising death of her brother – is married to Florizel, thus securing his rule in both countries. As Macbeth before them Leontes and Polixenes create sovereigns by trying to kill, or abandon, them.[512]

A related subject of interest for analysing *The Winter's Tale* is the ongoing education of a monarch, in this case Leontes, already observed in *Measure for Measure*. Shakespeare plays seem to indicate that the process of education for a monarch is not brought to an end – as claimed by King James – in the early years of his reign, but must be seen as a *lifelong process*[513] of learning how not to abuse power. This process is of course conducted in parts by faithful and loyal counsellors, like Escalus, or in this unusual case, Paulina, while

---

[507] Grene, David; *Reality and the Heroic Pattern. Last Plays of Ibsen, Shakespeare, and Sophocles.*; pp. 69

[508] Grene, David; *Reality and the Heroic Pattern. Last Plays of Ibsen, Shakespeare, and Sophocles.*; pp. 71

[509] *You know your father's temper: at this time / He will allow no speech [...]* (IV, 4, 447-48)

[510] see Snyder, Susan; *Introduction*; pp. 20

[511] *This brat is none of mine; / It is the issue of Polixenes.* (II, 3, 93-94)

[512] *From my succession wipe me, father; I / Am heir to my affection.* (IV, 4, 460-61)

[513] Snyder, Susan; *Introduction*; pp. 21

the refusal of advice and reasoned arguments counts as a the mark of a tyrant.[514]

The dangers and nature of tyranny has of course been discussed at length in *Macbeth*, so its reappearance in this late phase of Shakespeare's work process could be of some interest. King James distinction of course was very clear on this subject:

> *That whereas the proud and ambitious tyrant does think his kingdom and people are only ordained for satisfaction of his desires and unreasonable appetites, the righteous and just king does by the contrary acknowledge himself to be ordained the procuring of the wealth and prosperity of his people [...]*[515]

Yet Leontes does not directly remind the reader and audience of King James and it would seem that all implications are avoided by the ancient, distant, foreign design of the setting. Furthermore, Leontes' motivation stays, in most parts, a question for production. One could have him entering the stage already suspicious, hinting at a longer line of incidents during the mentioned nine months of Polixenes' stay, taking into account his insistence to be away so quickly now that the queen is visibly pregnant.[516]

But on the other hand one could also interpret his jealousy as a kind of tidal wave, suddenly seizing him, like the rage of Othello. The variations of production could impose upon him countless personalities, varying from righteous cuckold to deluded madman:

> *This jealousy / Is for a precious creature. As she's rare / Must it be great; and as his person's mighty, / Must it be violent; [...]* (I, 2, 445-48)

This ambiguity is indeed highly reminiscent of Duke Vincentio and it will have to be seen later if it has equal significance for the historical analysis. The debate about art and nature is dragged into this consideration of tyranny as Leontes expresses his hate and loathing for all pretence and artifice. As his rashness of jealousy and his long years of secluded grief cast the suspicion of unstableness upon his character, his objection to all theatrical behaviour and the

---

[514] *As or by oath remove or counsel shake / The fabric of his folly [...]* (I, 2, 423-24)
[515] Snyder, Susan; *Introduction*; pp. 22
[516] *Why, lo you know, I have spoken to th' purpose twice: / The one for I ever earned a royal husband, / Th' other, for some while a friend.* (I, 2, 105-107)

'show-act' of Hermione's trial he initiates cast doubt upon his honesty.[517]
The trial scene – the third in four analysed plays – is again of some importance for the play, as well as for the historical analysis. It has been stated before that the two female figures directly related to Leontes, Hermione and Perdita, equal each other in their demure, yet dignified, resignation in the face of their 'destiny'. While Hermione refuses to defend herself before a court that will call her adulteress, Perdita is silent in the presence of Polixenes and turns away from her 'false hopes':

> *I told you what would come of this. Beseech you, / Of your own state take care; This dream of mine [...] I'll queen it no inch farther [...]* (IV, 4, 426-29).

The trial itself is interrupted by the messengers of the oracle, the supreme appeal beyond any human law. In his refusal to obey this godly counsel, again resisting the force of reason, Leontes is forced to pay *a child for a child*[518], his punishment for abandoning Perdita even before the trial of her mother has already started and thus underlines his reduction of the law to a mere theatrical show effect. Many critics have linked this proceedings to the other trials conducted against queens throughout the Tudor age – Catherine of Aragon, Anne Boleyn and Mary Stuart – and it will have to be seen if these connection can be justified.

Lastly the play is of course a series of tests and trials for love and virtue, as *The Merchant of Venice* had been. Leontes fails his first test by misinterpreting the 'hand-holding' in Act I, Polixenes goes wrong in interrupting the 'hand-fasting' in Act IV, but all sins are redeemed by Hermione's 'hand-taking' in Act V.[519] The coming-alive of the statue is carefully prepared, leaving open both possibilities of miracle and show.

Paulina's mentioned 'excursions' to a far-flung house and Hermione's explanation that she has preserved herself for her daughter hint at a reasonable, if implausible, plan carried out by the

---

[517] *Let us be cleared / Of being tyrannous, since we so openly / Proceed in justice, which shall have due course / Even to her guilt, or the purgation.* (III, 2, 3-6)

[518] Grene, David; *Reality and the Heroic Pattern. Last Plays of Ibsen, Shakespeare, and Sophocles.*; pp. 80

[519] see Snyder, Susan; *Introduction*; pp. 23

two women over 16 years. Yet Paulina's show of mysticism[520] and her harsh interruption of her mistress' explanation[521] seem to indicate that the possibility of miracles should not be fully excluded from the play.

The figure of Time, impersonated by a quasi ancient chorus, appears in this context as the counterpart to the oracle – *cryptic and all-knowing*.[522] This Time reminds of the old gods of Fate, Justice, or Fortune, so frequently embedded in the ancient classics.[523]

Indeed, however, in *The Winter's Tale* the passage of time is both a threat concerning succession, death and decay, and a blessing bringing forth pregnancy, growth and the change of seasons. Only the process of ageing has something of both – the nearing adulthood of Perdita enabling a secure succession, while the wrinkles on Hermione's face speak of lost years.

---

[520] *It is required / You do awake your faith.* (V, 3, 94-95)
[521] *There's time enough for that,* (V, 3, 128)
[522] Snyder, Susan; *Introduction*; pp. 37
[523] *[...] since it is in my power / To o'erthrow law [...]* (IV, 1, 7-8)

Shepherds, Women and Courtiers

The thematic and plot-driven concern with succession and an underlying interrogation of monarchical power are perhaps the clearest links between The Winter's Tale *and the history play as Shakespeare defined it.*[524]

In the first part of *The Winter's Tale* it would seem that the audience is taken once more to see the development and consequence of a tyrant's reign. Leontes in his rage and confusion is surrounded – unlike Macbeth – with trusted counsellors, yet deaf to their pursuits of reason.[525] Denying this kind of 'rescue' in the first half of the play, he naturally suffers the same kind of destructive consequences Macbeth had to bear: the death of his son, wife and abandoned daughter and the loss of his friend Polixenes.[526]
Only the persistence and harsh commands of Paulina do, it seems, appeal to his better nature.[527] Feminist criticism points out that the plays steadily features desperate and confused men, either through love or grief, that are confronted with the eloquence and argumentative power of women – Leontes in his encounters with Hermione and Paulina, Polixenes and Florizel through their encounter with Perdita.[528] *The link between women's power of speech and their control of stage space is clearly set out in* The Winter's Tale.[529]
Therefore Leontes asks his queen to persuade his friend, when no other tongue would change his decision[530] and then can not stand her

---

[524] Snyder, Susan; *Introduction*; pp. 20
[525] *O that ever I / Had squared me to thy counsel!* (V, 1, 51-52).
[526] *[...] forget your evil; / With them, forgive yourself. [...] which was so much, / that heirless it hath made my kingdom [...]* (V, 1, 5-10).
[527] *Thou didst speak but well / When most the truth, which I receive much better / Than to be pitied of thee* (III, 2, 229-31).
[528] *[...] a lady's 'verily''s / As potent as a lord's.* (I, 2, 49-50)
[529] Bennett, Alexandra G. 2006. "Testifiying in the Court of Public Opinion: Margaret Cavendish Reworks *The Winter's Tale*." In: Romack, Katherine; Fitzmaurice, James (eds.). *Cavendish and Shakespeare, Interconnections*. Aldershot: Ashgate Publishing Company. pp. 85-102.; pp. 89
[530] *There is no tongue that moves, none, none i'th world [...] Tongue-tied our queen? Speak you.* (I, 2, 20-27)

successes.[531] *Leontes refutes her, not with logic or reason, but with reiterations and recriminations [...]*[532 and thus] Hermione is discarded easily, reminiscent of King Henry's queens. But the female force of argument stays with Leontes, who fears the kind of truth hurled at him by Paulina.[533]

The character of Paulina raises the question, who is able and willing to tell a monarch the truth and demonstrates how the bringer of unwelcome facts can be received.[534] Yet the argument has often been raised that, in listening to Paulina's advice concerning his remarriage, Leontes is as much misled as he was when abandoning his wife. It is probable that Paulina would try to avoid a remarriage of the king, if she knew that Hermione was still alive, yet from Leontes' perspective, leaving his kingdom without an heir constitutes a danger for the state and the natural order:

> *You pity not the state, nor the remembrance, / Of his most sovereign name; consider little / What dangers by his highness' fail of issue / May drop upon his kingdom [...]* (V, 1, 25-28).

Paulina's discharge of this argument:

> *Care not for issue; / The crown will find an heir. Great Alexander / Left his to th' worthiest; so his successor / Was like to be the best.* (V, 1, 46-49)

strikes the reader as odd and careless and must have been even more awkward for an early Jacobean audience, which had suffered through decades of uncertain succession, first under the child Edward, than the 'Spanish' Mary and finally the childless Elisabeth.

The Winter's Tale *is a story of [...] a king who is disordered both personally and politically by tremendous passions.*[535] Therefore, the question arises if the description of the royal house of Sicilia could

---

[531] *I have* tremor cordis *in me: my heart dances, / But not for joy.* (I, 2, 109-10).
[532] Bennett, Alexandra G. 2006. "Testifiying in the Court of Public Opinion: Margaret Cavendish Reworks *The Winter's Tale.*"; pp. 90
[533] *Antigonus, / I charged thee that she should not come about me [...]* (II, 3, 41-42).
[534] *Fear you his tyrannous passion more, alas, / Than the Queen's life?* (II, 3, 27-28)
[535] Zurcher, Amelia. 2003. "Untimely Monuments: Stoicism, History, and the Problem of Utility in The Winter's Tale." In: Ferguson, Frances (ed.). *English Literary History*. Baltimore, Maryland: Johns Hopkins Univ. Press, Vol. 70. pp. 903-925.; pp. 909

not have been intended to reflect upon a king's relation to his counsellors.[536]

King James of course was, it would seem, very susceptible to influences issued by his favourites and perhaps Leontes' absolute trust in Paulina's counsel should reflect on this kind of deliberateness, unfitting a monarch. King James' most trusted advisor in the time after his accession had been Robert Cecil, Queen Elisabeth's Secretary of State. Yet Cecil's influence on the king was decreasing since he had failed to procure the necessary assistance for James in the first serious struggle with Parliament in 1610. As has been mentioned before, the king was finally forced to dismiss the Parliament without having been granted the financial support he desperately needed.

Yet the issues underlying James's [...] relationships with his counsellors appear to inform the essentially realistic treatment of political relationships, depicted in The Winter's Tale.[537]

The royal prerogative for example, so carefully guarded by James, is brought forth by Leontes to support his insistence for justice and a public trial against all advice.[538] The 'natural goodness' of a divine king is of course cast into ironical light by Leontes' tyranny, but Hermione's defence of his supreme will[539] and her defence even of his character[540] seems to indicate yet again that tyrants as Leontes are not born, but made in the strain of their office.[541]

The king's will and prerogative was of course a tentative subject during James' reign, as was his ability to judge characters, as the

---

[536] see Kurland, Stuart M. 1991. "We need no more of your advice: Political Realism in *The Winter's Tale*." In: Patten, Robert L.(ed.). *Studies in English Literature 1500-1900*. Houston, Texas: Johns Hopkins University Press, Vol. 31. pp. 365-381.; pp. 365

[537] Kurland, Stuart M.; "We need no more of your advice": *Political Realism in* The Winter's Tale.; pp. 366

[538] *Our prerogative / Calls not your counsels, but our natural goodness / Imparts this [...]* (II, 1, 163-65)

[539] *Beseech you all, my lords, / With thoughts so qualified as your charities / Shall best instruct you, measure me; and so / The king's will be performed.* (II, 1, 111-14)

[540] *She's an adulteress! – Should a villain say so, / The most replenished villain in the world, / He were as much more villain. You my lord, / Do but mistake.* (II, 1, 76-80)

[541] *Thou dost advise me / Even so as mine own course have set down.* (I, 2, 336-37)

Raleigh trial has shown. In a speech before dismissing the Parliament in 1610 he had just underlined his absolute refusal to be advised or counselled by the congregation: *Kings are iustly called Gods [...] I must not be taught my Office [...].*[542]

This discharge of the official role of the Parliament caused a new uproar of indignation among the delegates and the claims of James' misuse of power and supposed secret intentions to turn England into an absolutistic regime were issued once more. Yet at this early stage of the public struggle for power between Parliament and crown, the blame fell mostly upon James' counsellors and favourites, as the misuse of power was believed to be most frequently based on opportunist courtiers, or as Shakespeare puts it:

> *You are abused, and by some putter-on / That will be damned for't; Would I knew the villain, / I would land-damn him!* (II, 1, 141-143)

This kind of conviction had already been expressed by Shakespeare himself in *Richard II*, but also in Thomas More's *Utopia*[543], in the *Basilikon Doron* itself - *take good head to the choice of your servants*[544] - or more broadly in Machiavelli's *Prince* – *flatterers are to be avoided.*[545] King James did unfortunately not take heed of his own advice in the years after 1610, when the fall from grace of Robert Cecil gave rise to his new favourite Robert Carr, who was disliked and mistrusted in London even before the Overbury scandal. In *The Winter's Tale*, Hermione's death gives rise to another female counsellor, *the power that Hermione once wielded through words passes to Paulina,*[546] who declares herself to be the only one, to tell Leontes the truth about his behaviour and is threatened with torture:

> *What studied torments, tyrant, hast for me? / What wheels? racks? fires? What flaying? boiling? In leads or oils? What old or newer torture / Must I receive [...]* (III, 2, 172-74)

---

[542] Kurland, Stuart M.; "We need no more of your advice": *Political Realism in* The Winter's Tale.; pp. 367

[543] see Kurland, Stuart M.; "We need no more of your advice": *Political Realism in* The Winter's Tale.; p 368

[544] Kurland, Stuart M.; "We need no more of your advice": *Political Realism in* The Winter's Tale.; pp. 369

[545] Kurland, Stuart M.; "We need no more of your advice": *Political Realism in* The Winter's Tale.; pp. 369

[546] Bennett, Alexandra G.; *Testifiying in the Court of Public Opinion:* pp. 93

The king's first advisor Camillo, *who serves first Leontes and then Polixenes, each of whom declares himself absolutely dependent upon Camillo's counsel*,[547] is the first to realise the dangerous state in which Leontes will put himself and all around him:

> *I must be the poisoner / Of good Polixenes, and my ground to do't / Is the obedience to a master, one / Who, in rebellion with himself, will have / All that are his so too.* (I, 2, 348-52)

But he indeed also serves as another example to show how little difference there really is between the court of Sicilia and Bohemia, when Polixenes grows as dependent of him, than Leontes had been before:

> *I pray thee, good Camillo, be no more importunate. 'Tis a sickness denying thee anything, a death to grant this. [...] The need I have of thee thine own goodness hath made.* (IV, 2, 1-10)

And he is nevertheless inclined to 'betray' both his masters for his own sake. Paulina in contrast to him is an unusual counsellor to a king, firstly because she is a woman and secondly because she holds no official position at court, now that she is no longer required to serve her 'dead' queen. Her *lack of self-control*[548] makes her an even more unusual character and stresses her equality to Leontes, Polixenes, or even Florizel, whom not even good Camillo can advise against his will.[549]

Because of her lack of office Paulina would of course present herself as the kind of un-opportunistic advisor so rarely found by any ruler, but on the other hand she is depicted as politically inexperienced in the 'succession debate'.[550] Her persistence in letting Leontes suffer for his sins:

> *But, O thou tyrant, / Do not repent these things, for they are heavier / Than all thy woes can stir; therefore betake thee / To nothing but despair.* (III, 2, 204-207)

---

[547] Kurland, Stuart M.; "We need no more of your advice": *Political Realism in* The Winter's Tale.; pp. 373

[548] Kurland, Stuart M.; "We need no more of your advice": *Political Realism in* The Winter's Tale.; pp. 376

[549] *Be advised. – I am, and by my fancy. If my reason, / Will thereto be obedient, I have reason; / If not, my senses, better pleased with madness, / Do bid it welcome.* (IV, 4, 460-65)

[550] *What, sovereign sir, / I did not well, I meant well [...]* (V, 3, 2-3)

could easily have led to a desperate fate like Pandosto's, exemplifying once more that good intentions are not enough to rule a kingdom. Yet she never loses the directorship of the action, leading up to Hermione's resurrection, reminding the reader far more of Vincentio, than the sad Leontes does in this second half and, like in *Measure for Measure*, *Again, the happy outcome [...] comes about fortuitously, even miraculously.*[551]

Another topic of relevance for the historical analysis of the play presents itself in the before mentioned contrast of country and court and the development of this distinction depicted in *The Winter's Tale*. Jacobean London at the time of King James' accession had developed into a *suburban metropolis*[552], reaching out far beyond its walls, and thus into a challenge for the traditional distinction of town and country. These distinction Shakespeare himself presented so traditionally in plays like *As You Like It*, seems to be preserved in *The Winter's Tale* only in one long scene, namely the 'sheep-shearing' in Act IV, scene 4, where Perdita presides over a tableau of traditional pastoral figures as a kind of rural goddess:

[...] no shepherdess, but Flora / Peering in April's front [...] Is as a meeting of the pretty gods, / And you the queen on't.
(IV, 4, 1-5)

Yet, as has been mentioned before, the play seems not interested in preserving this kind of idyll, but distorts it into a battle ground for Polixenes and his son.

The 'reaching out' of the city of London beyond its medieval boundaries was naturally an important development for the theatres, who had – both socially and geographically – occupied a *marginal*[553] space, outside the city walls or on special ground within to avoid confrontation with the Puritans and authorities. Through the mass increase of population and the vast growth of the 'urban sprawl', however, the theatres found themselves in the early 17th century in the middle of the actual town of London, whose 'outwalled' section

---

[551] Kurland, Stuart M.; "We need no more of your advice": *Political Realism in* The Winter's Tale.; pp. 378

[552] Horton, Craig. 2003. "...the country must diminish: Jacobean London and the Production of Pastoral Space in *The Winter's Tale*." In: Australian & New Zealand Association for Medieval and Early Modern Studies. *Parergon*. Canberra: Univ. of West. Australia Press, Vol. 20. pp. 85-107.; pp. 85

[553] Horton, Craig; *Jacobean London and the Production of Pastoral Space in* The Winter's Tale.; pp. 90

suddenly *actually accommodated the majority of London's population and constituted some two-thirds of its geographical area.*[554]
The official authorities naturally watched this kind of development with caution and anticipation, for they feared a decrease of rural communities and a centralisation on London that would soon depopulate the agrarian regions. King James himself addressed the problem in one of his speeches before the troubled Parliament of 1610: *[...] but the country must diminish, if London does so increase.*[555]
The common fear was that England would soon be nothing more than the city of London, which nevertheless depended on all the rest of the country to provide for its food and commodities. Thus the productions of pastoral space in the English renaissance had pictured the rural areas as a mixture of the biblical Eden and the pagan 'Golden Age' proclaimed by poets like Ovid or Virgil.[556] Shakespeare included some of these references, as shall be shown in the next chapter, but nevertheless his pastoral scene in *The Winter's Tale* stands apart from his earlier productions, where the peace and quiet of the fields or woods had provided a refuge from the problems of the court:

> a *contrast between the 'natural' and 'human' worlds; the organicism, democracy [...] and honesty of rural life, versus the artificiality, hierarchical complexity [...] and cultured order of the city/court.*[557]

The position of the sheep-shearing scene within the plot hints at first at this kind of refuge, providing a secure and sheltered home for the abandoned princess. But then the difference between Bohemia and Sicilia collapses with Polixenes' appearance and history repeats itself – the prince is abandoned and even Camillo's flight is replayed. The peaceful realm of Bohemia thus turns into a mirror of the Sicilia of 16 years previously and intensifies the conflicts of the play, rather

---

[554] Horton, Craig; *Jacobean London and the Production of Pastoral Space in* The Winter's Tale.; pp. 91

[555] Horton, Craig; *Jacobean London and the Production of Pastoral Space in* The Winter's Tale.; pp. 92

[556] see Horton, Craig; *Jacobean London and the Production of Pastoral Space in* The Winter's Tale.; pp. 94

[557] Horton, Craig; *Jacobean London and the Production of Pastoral Space in* The Winter's Tale.; pp. 94

than providing a solution. While these contortions happen, however, the outward signs of the pastoral are kept – the clown, the shepherds and shepherdesses, the seasonal feast, music and dance – even though natural danger, the bear, and human danger, Autolycus, cast still further doubt upon the harmony:[558] *With die and drab I purchased this caparison, and my revenue is the silly cheat.*[559]
In its description of the two rulers of Sicilia and Bohemia in the very first act, the similarity of their personalities, and thus their kingdoms, is already foreshadowed, as Leontes and Polixenes have been educated and raised together and thus most probably share equal convictions and beliefss:

> *Since their more mature dignities and royal necessities made separation of their society, their encounters, though not personal, hath been royally attorney with interchange of gifts, letters, loving embassies [...]* (I, 1, 21-24)

Yet Polixenes' childhood memories evoke a kind of lost era [560] impossible to recall, for it was lost through temptation.[561]
This strange coincidence of biblical images, Eden the fall of man, and the queen as the tempting devil, could serve as an explanation for the motiveless tyranny of Leontes and Polixenes that destroys and disrupts both countries and decrease the pastoral refuge to a kind of brief sanctuary. The loss of innocence in its king would, in a sense of body politic, naturally lose the kingdom's paradise innocence as well. Perhaps Shakespeare intended the biblical impact to be related to the diminishing country outside London, but if this criticism was directed at the romantic sentimentalism preserved by plays like *Pandosto*, opting for a new and modern approach, or if he blamed the king for not preserving this kind of idyll, it is hard to decide.
There is another social distinction in the play, however, that does relate to this problem. As has been shown before, the social class system of England was much more permeable than most others in

---

[558] see Horton, Craig; *Jacobean London and the Production of Pastoral Space in The Winter's Tale.*; pp. 97
[559] IV, 3, 26-27
[560] *What we changed / Was innocence for innocence;* (I, 2, 67-68)
[561] *Temptations have since then been born to's: for / In those unfledged days was my wife a girl; / Your precious self had then not crossed the eyes / Of my young playfellow. – Grace to boot! / Of this make no conclusion, lest you say / Your queen and I are devils.* (I, 2, 76-81)

Europe, and yet *The Winter's Tale* still expresses a kind of class prejudice concerning the difference between town and country:

> *[...] he is seldom from the house of a most homely shepherd, a man, they say, that from very nothing, and beyond the imagination of his neighbours, is grown into an unspeakable estate.* (IV, 2, 30-33)

The uneasiness about a mere shepherd accumulating this kind of wealth reflects upon the anxiety of the citizens and courtiers, who had been hard pressed to accept merchants and adventurers into their ranks, but were uneasy about the decline of feudal systems and the freehold of agrarian estates.[562] Florizel is a *dangerous merger*[563] in these affairs, as he is much more comfortable with his disguise and his mingling with the shepherds and farmers than Perdita is:

> *Your high self, / The gracious mark o'th'land, you have obscured / With a swain's wearing, and me, poor lowly maid, / most goddess-like pranked upp. [...] To me the difference forges dread;* (IV, 4, 7-17).

Although Florizel never loses his authority and standing, even in the pastoral dance, and Perdita seems to have inherited a kind of aristocratic bearing,[564] Polixenes is not willing to allow such a dangerous misalliance.[565] The power of the king exposes himself in much the same kind of tyranny that his friend Leontes applied against his daughter, endangering his kingdom and destabilising his own succession by abandoning his only son, rather than allowing him to marry a shepherdess:

> *[...] thou a sceptre's heir [...] I am sorry that by hanging thee I can / But shorten thy life one week. [...] I'll have thy beauty scratched with briers and made you more homely than thy state. [...] we'll bar thee from succession, / Not hold thee of our blood, [...]* (IV, 4, 398-410)

Both Florizel and Perdita, though unknowingly, are trespassers in a society where they do not belong and thus the production of pastoral

---

[562] see Horton, Craig; *Jacobean London and the Production of Pastoral Space in* The Winter's Tale.; pp. 102

[563] Horton, Craig; *Jacobean London and the Production of Pastoral Space in* The Winter's Tale.; pp. 103

[564] *But smacks of something greater than herself, / Too noble for this place.* (IV, 4, 158-59)

[565] *Your resolution can not hold when 'tis / Opposed, as it must be, by th'power of the King.* (IV, 4, 35-36)

space in *The Winter's Tale* turns into a social conflict that not even Camillo can argue away.[566]

Florizel in his suiting role as dedicated lover of course realizes, what both Leontes and Polixenes do not – that the love of an office never equals the love of your wife:

> *That were I crowned the most imperial monarch / Thereof most worthy, were I the faintest youth / That ever made eye swerve [...] I would not prize them / Without her love [...]* (IV, 4, 351-55).

But still the danger for the personal bodies of Florizel and Perdita, and the reflected dangers for the body politics of Sicilia and Bohemia are only lifted through Leontes late acknowledgement of his daughter. Thus the court, and not the country, serves as the basis for solution and miracle, when Hermione's blessing makes every further conflict unthinkable. Perhaps this impossibility of separation between city and country, as both infouence each other constantly for better or worse, is the final message of the inclusion of pastoral space intended by Shakespeare.[567]

Yet philosophical criticism has inflicted upon this 'miracle', ending another contemporary renaissance debate – the question of value and virtue of stoicism, a fashionable idea of the Stuart age presenting *a blend of scepticism, Tacitism, and reason of state.*[568] Hermione and Perdita exemplify the restraint from emotion in their encounters with injustice; Paulina and Florizel demonstrate the opposite. King James had, in the *Basilikon Doron*, included the advice that a just ruler had to refrain from personal emotions while conducting the affairs of state[569], but in *The Winter's Tale* Hermione's stoicism becomes even ironical through her reappearance as a concrete statue. Leontes plays with this kind of imagery - *I am ashamed. Does not the stone rebuke me / For being more stone than it?*[570]

---

[566] *Besides, you know / Prosperity's the very bond of love, / Whose fresh complexion and whose heart together / Affliction alters.* (IV, 4, 551-54)

[567] Horton, Craig; *Jacobean London and the Production of Pastoral Space in* The Winter's Tale.; pp. 107

[568] Zurcher, Amelia; *Untimely Monuments: Stoicism, History, and the Problem of Utility in* The Winter's Tale.; pp. 910

[569] see Zurcher, Amelia; *Untimely Monuments: Stoicism, History, and the Problem of Utility in* The Winter's Tale.; pp. 910

[570] V, 3, 37-38

The cure of the king's grief and the new union of his marriage provide, in the sense of the body politic, naturally the healing of the whole kingdom, including in this case the stability of succession.[571] Reason and plausibility are clearly rejected in this miraculous ending, even if a probable explanation could be found by a careful reader – if probably not by a murmuring Jacobean audience. Yet it shall be analysed in the next chapter if the statue scene can really only bee seen as a kind of political *deus ex machina*, as applied by Duke Vincentio, or if there my be a more religious meaning to the wondrous recovery.

---

[571] *No settled senses of the world can match / The pleasure of that madness.* (V, 3, 72-73)

Leontes, Perdita and the Golden Age

> The Winter's Tale, *with its overall suspicion of reason and it's ultimate espousal of super-natural avenues to knowledge such as miracle, spectacle, and ritual, is a specimen of Counter-Reformation ideology and aesthetics.*[572]

As has been shown in the last chapters, *The Winter's Tale* includes some of the biblical and pagan images of a Garden of Eden or a Golden Age. The classic literature frequently dwelled on this fabled period of festivity and wealth, for example in the works of Ovid, Pliny or Cicero.[573] As these kind of classical references were often conferred to in the English renaissance, it is not surprising that King James was greeted upon his accession with jubilation and the hope that a new Golden Age was dawning after the difficult last years of Elisabeth's reign. *James was welcomed as a second Arthur [...] like a second Augustus [...].*[574]

The euphoria greeting the new monarch however was, as has been mentioned, short lived and already his first Parliaments in 1604 and 1606 were overshadowed by complaints about James' behaviour and political doctrines.[575] Shakespeare's plays of this time are frequently concerned with political matters, as has been shown in this essay, but in the case of *The Winter's Tale* these political allusions have so far been less noticeable than for example in *Macbeth* or *Measure for Measure*. This subtlety is also visible in the play's treatment of the 'Golden Age mythology'. Although the mythological land of Sicilia already invites this kind of ancient legendry, the harmony and

---

[572] Landau, Aaron. 2003. "No settled senses of the world can match the pleasure of that madness: The Politics of Unreason in The Winter's Tale." In: Institut de Recherches sur la Renaissance, l'Âge Classique et les Lumières. *Cahiers Élisabéthains*. Montpellier: A Biannual Journal of English Renaissance Studies. Univ. of Montpellier Press, Vol. 64. pp. 29-42.; pp. 30

[573] Hardman, C. B. 1994. "Shakespeare's *Winter's Tale* and the Stuart Golden Age." In: Bradshaw, David (ed.). *The Review of English Studies*. Oxford: Oxford Univ. Press, Vol. 45. pp. 221-229.; pp. 223

[574] Hardman, C. B. 1994. "Shakespeare's *Winter's Tale* and the Stuart Golden Age."; pp. 221

[575] see Hardman, C. B. 1994. "Shakespeare's *Winter's Tale* and the Stuart Golden Age."; pp. 222

abundance are quickly destroyed by the eccentric behaviour of Leontes, perhaps reminiscent of the decline in popularity James had to endure after his jubilant entrance to London. In antiquity it was believed that the goddess Astrea would be leaving the earth last, before the final collapse of the Golden Age, just like Perdita leaves Sicilia before the decline of her father's mental state and thus the kingdom's wealth and stability.[576] Astrea was, however, one of Elisabeth's alter egos, so her departure and the end of the Tudor era could well have been the end of the actual Golden Age for Shakespeare. The imagery connecting Perdita and Elisabeth, however, does not exhaust itself in the probably far-fetched analogy of Astrea, but also links Perdita to the virgin goddess Flora in the sheep-shearing scene. Like the return of spring, Perdita brings harmony and prosperity back to her home country and is reunited with her mother. Hermione's appeal meanwhile is targeted at the *god of shepherds and art*[577] Apollo, who incidentally also served as the patron of the classical Golden Age.

These allusions to the pagan form of paradise imagery are, however, accompanied by the Christian images of biblical paradise, and again it is the Catholic imagery that is most often commented on, because of Shakespeare's supposed *sympathy for the old faith*.[578] Already in the first scenes of the play Camillo is given a double role of advisor and priest:

> *I have trusted thee, Camillo / With all the nearest things to my heart, as well / My chamber-counsels, wherein, priest-like, thou / Hast cleansed my bosom: [...]* (I, 2, 132-35)

As will be Paulina, who is threatened with death and torture, while remaining morally steadfast:

> *A most unworthy and unnatural lord / Can do no more. – I'll ha' thee burnt. – I care not. / It is an heretic that makes the fire, / Not she which burns in't. I'll not call you tyrant; / But this most usage of you queen, [...]* (II, 3, 111-16)

This martyr imagery is supported by Leontes 'conversion' under her tutelage and her punishment for him, leaving him in grief and despair

---

[576] see Hardman, C. B.; *Shakespeare's* Winter's Tale *and the Stuart Golden Age*.; pp. 224

[577] Hardman, C. B.; *Shakespeare's* Winter's Tale *and the Stuart Golden Age*.; pp. 227

[578] Landau, Aaron; *The Politics of Unreason in* The Winter's Tale.; pp. 29

for 16 years.[579] Camillo's influence is later described as soothing and medical to the hot temper of Polixenes,[580] as again will be Paulina later on. The English renaissance believed that the main task of a healer was to secure the balance of the four humours in a body, and it is obvious before Paulina's intervention that the king's 'rebellion with himself' has caused errors in the balance of his body politic.[581] She refers to herself as 'physician' to the king,[582] although the reader does not know if this refers to the king's bodily or mental health or even the well-being of the body politic.

As Paulina's physician analogy [...] is aimed to cure those who structurally low (the rebellious daughter) or high (the tyrannical King) is premised on a harmony model of both the psyche and the state (which are analogues of each other).[583] Yet in a search for Catholic imagery the statue scene becomes immediately obvious. The kind of Counter-Reformation Raleigh, Southampton and also Shakespeare are associated with, was seeking a renewed form of mysticism, counterbalancing the 'scientific', rationalist religion proclaimed by the Calvinists and Puritans. The main assumption of this conviction was that all human knowledge is limited and therefore trying to unravel religious mysteries by rational thought a ridiculous endeavour.[584] In *The Winter's Tale*, critics have found this kind of anti-rationalism in the persistence of unreason, the frequent refusal of some characters – for example in Leontes or Florizel – to let themselves be governed by reason and the mysticism evoked by Paulina in the statue scene.[585]

---

[579] see Vanita, Ruth. 2000. "Mariological Memory in *The Winter's Tale* and *Henry VIII*." In: Patten, Robert L.(ed.). *Studies in English Literature 1500-1900*. Houston, Texas: Johns Hopkins University Press, Vol. 40. pp. 311-337.; pp. 318

[580] *Preserver of my father, now of me, / The medicine of our house [...]* (IV, 4, 566-67)

[581] see Gash, Anthony; *Shakespeare's Carnival and the Sacred*: The Winter's Tale *and* Measure for Measure.; pp. 194

[582] *Myself your loyal servant, your physician, / Your most obedient counsellor [...]* (II, 3, 54-55).

[583] Gash, Anthony; *Shakespeare's Carnival and the Sacred*: The Winter's Tale *and* Measure for Measure.; pp. 193

[584] see Landau, Aaron; *The Politics of Unreason in* The Winter's Tale.; pp. 30

[585] *And do not say 'tis superstition, that / I kneel and then implore her blessing.* (V, 3, 43-44)

The encouraging of superstitions was a criminal offence in Jacobean England[586] and the return of the prodigal daughter as a 'reward' for Leontes' 16 years of martyrdom and conversion to this kind of superstition, would seem to be even more of an offence. The play is seen in this context as a *series of baffling inconsistencies*[587] and the resurrection of Hermione as a full fledged Christian miracle.[588]
The blessing Perdita receives by her mother thus recalls the old idolism of saints and martyrs so fiercely rejected by the reformed church and *denounced as theatrical deception.*[589]
It seems only natural in this course of argument that Leontes *grounds his suspicions on both a Calvinistic belief that human nature is depraved because of the Fall, and an obsessive hatred for the theatre [...].*[590]
This kind of *antitheatricalism*[591] shown by Leontes, but also by Perdita before the statue scene, is a true example for Puritan resentments against the deceit of artificial behaviour. [592] *Reformation debates about the morality of festivity*[593], because rituals and seasonal feasts as celebrated in the sheep-shearing scene were considered to revoke the old 'papist' traditions and lead to a new 'outbreak' of idolatry and iconoclasm. Suspicions were naturally raised especially against the rural areas in the north of England, for their 'backwardness' and latent Catholicism were regarded a major threat

---

[586] see Vanita, Ruth; *Mariological Memory in* The Winter's Tale *and* Henry VIII.; pp. 321
[587] see Landau, Aaron; *The Politics of Unreason in* The Winter's Tale.; pp. 35
[588] *You gods look down, / And from your sacred vials pour your graces / Upon my daughter's head!* (V, 3, 122-23)
[589] see Hardman, C. B.; *Shakespeare's* Winter's Tale *and the Stuart Golden Age.*; pp. 37
[590] Moran, Andrew Damian. 2004. "The Chapel and the Gallery: Religion and Theatre in *The Winter's Tale.*" In: University Microfilms International. *Dissertation Abstracts International / A, The Humaniaties and Social Sciences.* Ann Arbor, Mich: UMI, Vol. 64. pp. 2501.; pp. 2501
[591] Moran, Andrew Damian. 2004. "The Chapel and the Gallery: Religion and Theatre in *The Winter's Tale.*"; pp. 2501
[592]*Come, quench your blushes, and present yourself / That which you are, Mistress o'th Feast.* (IV, 4, 66-67)
[593] Jensen, Phebe. 2004. "Singing Psalms to Horn-Pipes: Festivity, Iconoclasm and Chatholicism in *The Winter's Tale.*" In: Shakespeare Association of America. *Shakespeare Quarterly.* Washington D.C.: Folger Shakespeare Library, Vol. 55. pp. 279-306.; pp. 280

to the rest of the kingdom. Because of these unique circumstances defenders of traditional feast and pastimes found themselves accused of papist treason, while underground Catholics engaged themselves in the defence of traditional festivity.[594]

Leontes fear and hatred of spectacles[595] and ongoing suspicions of deceit are thus 'punished' in the end by him being rebuked by a false statue. Though *The Winter's Tale* is considered to be *not a Catholic play*[596], a kind of defence of the rural traditions can be found in the pastoral scene nevertheless.

King James himself published the *Book of Sports* in 1616, as a result of ceaseless debates about the morality of Sunday activities and old English traditions, like church wakes, Maypoles, bear beatings, theatre performances and athletic activities. Puritan conservatives of course refrained from all of these and protested against their legalisation, for all non-spiritual activities on a Sunday were supposed to unfocus the mind and possibly lead to 'papist' rituals.[597] The sheep-shearing evokes some of these rural traditions in a friendly and joyful festivity, including clowns, dances, singing and feasting.

In Act I, the accusations raised against Hermione are still full of hatred for theatrical behaviour[598] and the fear of plots and deceit. Leontes' ironical use of words like play - *Go play, boy, play: thy mother plays, and I / Play too, [...]*[599] - and sport also include him in the mistrust of all pastime activities, so innocently raised by Mamillius or even Camillo.[600]

---

[594] Jensen, Phebe. 2004. "Singing Psalms to Horn-Pipes: Festivity, Iconoclasm and Chatholicism in *The Winter's Tale*."; pp. 281

[595] *But to be paddling palms, and pinching fingers, / As now they are, and making practised smiles / As in a looking-glass, [...]* (I, 2, 114-16)

[596] Jensen, Phebe. 2004. "Singing Psalms to Horn-Pipes: Festivity, Iconoclasm and Chatholicism in *The Winter's Tale*."; pp. 282

[597] see Jensen, Phebe; *Singing Psalms to Horn-Pipes: Festivity, Iconoclasm and Chatholicism in* The Winter's Tale.; pp. 289

[598] *There is a plot against my life, my crown. / All's true that is mistrusted. [...] a very trick / For them to play at will.* (II, 1, 47-52)

[599] I, 2, 185-86

[600] *To satisfy your highness, and the entreaties / Of our most gracious mistress. – Satisfy? / Th' entreaties of your mistress? Satisfy?* (I, 2, 129-31)

Perdita shows a more subdued uneasiness in her role as mistress of the feast and voices with wonder the possibility that such an office might indeed change one's character:
Meethinks I play as I have seen them do, / In Whitsun pastorals: sure this robe of mine / Does change my disposition.[601]
Her 'accusation' of the flowers[602] becomes ironical considering her own supposed bastardry – *the flower may be no more a bastard than Perdita herself.*[603]
More direct allusions to the reformation undertaken by Henry VIII, his wives and his breach with Rome are supposed to be represented by the martial conflicts of Leontes and Hermione, which give another importance to Perdita's bastardry and her assumed connection to Elisabeth. A direct naming of these religious conflicts on stage would of course have been impossible because of the law of 1599, but the topic of the reign of Henry VIII, his queens and reformations became a fashionable topic for historical recreation in the early Stuart age[604], as seen in Shakespeare's own play *Henry VIII*.
In *The Winter's Tale* critics have 'found' the struggle of the King's Great Matter in the constellation of Leontes, Hermione and Polixenes, relating them to Henry, Catherine and Arthur. Of course such a relation seems to present itself, considering that King Henry thought to dispose of his infertile wife by a charge that was all but adultery.[605]
His claim that no marriage between him and Catherine could ever have been legitimate, when she had been legally married to his brother before him, was nevertheless considered as insubstantial as Leontes ravings.[606] His shocking procedure to have a queen be brought to a public trial to testify, caused outrage on Catherine's behalf in London, the more as her 'successor' Anne was not at all

---

[601] IV, 4, 131-34
[602] *[...] the fairest flowers o'th season [...] Which some call nature's bastards* (IV, 4, 81-84)
[603] Jensen, Phebe. 2004. "Singing Psalms to Horn-Pipes: Festivity, Iconoclasm and Chatholicism in *The Winter's Tale*."; pp. 300
[604] see Landau, Aaron; *The Politics of Unreason in* The Winter's Tale.; pp. 30
[605] *No court in Europe is too good for thee; / What dost thou then in prison?* (II, 2, 2-3)
[606] *[...] for as she hath / Been publicly accused, so shall she have / A just and open trial.* (II, 3, 202-204)

popular. Catherine's dignified refusal to surrender to a court that should prove her marriage illegal after so many years, greatly diminished the king's popularity as well, but even before Anne Boleyn's time there had been considerations concerning a re-marriage of the king for successions sake.[607]

This is of course a reversal of the action in *The Winter's Tale*, where the son dies out of desperation about the fate of his mother, who is unjustly subjected to trial. Yet the unjustness of accusation and trial would hold true for both Catherine and Anne, and Hermione strangely seems to carry strands of both characters. On the one hand, she is of course the dignified and highly aristocratic queen Catherine had been:

> *A fellow of the royal bed, which owe / A moiety of the throne, a great king's daughter, / The mother to a hopeful prince, here standing / To prate and talk for life and honour 'fore* (III, 2, 35-39)

but on the other her claims that her second child is murdered and she herself called a whore, would be more fitting for Anne's case, who had indeed been called 'the great whore' even in her days as queen, and had lost her second child in a miscarriage:

> *My second joy, / And first-fruit of my body, from my presence / I am barred like one infectious. My third comfort, / Starred most unluckily, is from my breast [...] Haled out to murder; myself on every post / Proclaimed a strumpet; [...]* (III, 2, 94-100)

Both women were of course separated from their daughters and both pleaded innocence, even though in Catherine's case there was hardly anything she could be guilty of, as no one would ever have levelled the kind of accusations against her that Anne had to endure.[608]

Indeed, as has been elaborated before, even Queen Anne's guilt was also more than questionable and her trial was considered, even by contemporaries, more a show than justice, again something she shares with Hermione.[609] Catherine died in her exile, while Queen

---

[607] *If the king had no son, they would desire to live on crutches till he had one.* (I, 1, 39-40)

[608] *[...] it shall scarce boot me / To say, 'not guilty'; mine integrity, Being counted falsehood, shall as I express it / Be so received.* (III, 2, 23-26)

[609] *When you shall know your mistress / Has deserved prison, then abound in tears / As I come out.* (II, 1, 119-21)

Anne was beheaded on the king's command. Thus the line accusing Leontes – *If one by one you wedded all the world [...] she you killed / Would be unparalleled.*[610] – would be fitting for King Henry in both, and more, cases.
Ironically:
> The Winter's Tale *and* Henry VIII *are built on a paradox – their women protagonists acquire increased moral authority even while they are being demoted and persecuted.*[611]

The trial of Hermione is often related to the trial of Queen Catherine in *King Henry VIII*. The story of *The Winter's Tale*, however, unfolds quite differently form the historical original, when Hermione decides to separate from her husband of her own free will, rather then being abandoned, and yet she *bemoans the fact that [...] she can be so easily [...] threatened with death.*[612] This recalls perfectly the 'un-queening' of Catherine and Anne under Henry VIII, even though the two seem to get mixed up in the person of Hermione.

Camillo, who is not to be persuaded of his queen's guilt in this analogy becomes Henry's own chancellor Thomas More, who was unable to procure him the annulment of his marriage and the oracle would naturally represent the Vatican[613], from whom Henry had hoped to secure the legalisation of his annulment, but received only the assurance that he was indeed legally married.

Leontes rage and the refusal to accept this statement[614] mirror more than anything else in the play Henry's break with the Pope, who could be interpreted as a kind of Christian equivalent to the Oracle of Delphi. Thomas More was executed in due course along with many others, because he could not set his sovereigns will above his own conscience – an offence that neither Henry nor Leontes could lightly

---

[610] V, 1, 14-16

[611] Vanita, Ruth; *Mariological Memory in* The Winter's Tale *and* Henry VIII.; pp. 311

[612] Vanita, Ruth; *Mariological Memory in* The Winter's Tale *and* Henry VIII.; pp. 315

[613] *Now from the oracle / They will bring all, whose spiritual counsel had / Shall stop or spur me.* (II, 1, 184-86)

[614] *There is no truth in all i'th oracle. / The session shall proceed; this is mere falsehood.* (III, 2, 137-38)

tolerate and which made both of them even more determined to have their will.⁶¹⁵

Henry's jealousy in the case of Anne Boleyn has often been called false, a theatrical act, played to rid him of a queen who had failed to bring forth male offspring and who was replaced *ad hoc* by her own lady in waiting – though in a more bodily sense than Hermione is replaced at Leontes' court by the admonishing presence of Paulina:

> *[...] Is this nothing? / Why then the world and all that's in't is nothing / The covering sky is nothing, Bohemia nothing, / My wife is nothing, not nothing have these nothings, / If this be nothing.* (I, 2, 289-93)

The fate of Hermione and her resemblance to King Henry's unfortunate queens brings the argument back to Elisabeth and Perdita. Although it is true that the lines telling of Hermione's separation from her daughter would have been fitting for Mary as well, who was forced away from her mother's side by will of her father, the before mentioned allusions linking Perdita to Flora and Astrea, however, leave little doubt that she is more likely to recall Elisabeth's image than Mary's:

> *This child was prisoner to the womb and is / By law and process of great nature thence / Freed and enfranchised, not a party to / The anger of the King, nor guilty of / (If any be) the trespass of the Queen.* (II, 2, 57-61)

Elisabeth too shares Perdita's fate of abandonment by her own father, declaration of bastardy and her miraculous survival to return to power after her brother's death. In Act V, Perdita is even associated with religious 'power', as Elisabeth had been, when she and her Parliament were designing the Elizabethan Settlement.⁶¹⁶ As a new idol for her subjects she is bringing a new Golden Age to Sicilia,⁶¹⁷ as Elisabeth had brought to England after the disrupted mid-Tudor crisis.

---

⁶¹⁵*Camillo and Polixenes / Laugh at me, make their pastime at my sorrow; / They should not laugh if I could reach them, nor / Shall she, within my power.* (II, 3, 23-26)

⁶¹⁶*This is a creature, / Would she begin a sect, might quench the zeal / Of all professors else, make proselytes* (V, 1, 106-109)

⁶¹⁷*Women will love her that she is a woman / More worth than any man; men, that she is / The rarest of all women.* (V, 1, 110-12)

Almost always it is only in a work of fiction that irrational and murderous tyranny or treachery can be resolved in personal, dynastic and political harmony.[618]

---

[618] Hardman, C. B.; *Shakespeare's* Winter's Tale *and the Stuart Golden Age.*; pp. 228

Conclusion

James I of England c. 1606
Portrait by John de Critz

Summary

> *It is often, as if the plays inform Shakespeare as much as Shakespeare informs the plays.*[619]

In the course of this essay it has been shown that Shakespeare not only relied on a variety of contemporary and classical sources for the composition of his plays, but that he was interested and involved in contemporary social and political debates and, being *genuinely engaged with political issues of importance in his world,*[620] frequently embedded them in his work.
In the first play discussed, *The Merchant of Venice*, this kind of political interest may be at first difficult to observe, as it is the only play in this analysis not directly engaged in questions of sovereignty. Yet *had his premise been wholly imaginary, his treatment could easily have been relatively free of contradiction.*[621]
The social problem of the divided Church of England may be found in the encounter of Shylock and Antonio, and it may also well be a criticism, if not of the Elizabethan Settlement as a whole, of the Protestant or Puritan hypocrisy, shown in Venice's treatment of the Jew. Indeed it would, however, be partial to imprint the 'victim' part on Shylock, who shows as much hypocrisy in the trial scene and has to be reminded by Portia that no man is without fail. This first trial scene thus exemplifies the unwillingness of all analysed plays to favour one argument, or one 'side' of propaganda completely. Shylock's and Antonio's hatred is mutual, their positions entrenched, neither free of sin, nor of hypocrisy. This is the description of the religious situation in Venice Shakespeare provides, and if we assume this position to be a reflection of England, it is hard to argue that he possibly favoured either position.
The second topic of importance discussed in *The Merchant of Venice* relates more directly to the question of royal sovereignty. In

---

[619] Barrol, Leeds; *Politics, Plague and Shakespeare's Theatre. The Stuart Years.*; pp. 1
[620] Kurland, Stuart M.; "We need no more of your advice": *Political Realism in* The Winter's Tale.; pp. 379
[621] Cohen, Walter; The Merchant of Venice *and the Possibilities of Historical Criticism.*; pp. 774

the descriptions of love relationships in the play there have been found many critical insides into the Elizabethan society – the promiscuity suggested by the ring plot, the confusion of power, wealth and love observed in Bassanio and Lorenzo and the 'suitability-test' staged for Portia's suitors. It has been argued that Portia should be considered as the main character of the play and that she shows considerable similarities to Queen Elisabeth. Yet this comparison has its advantages as well as drawbacks. Her circle of wooers, to which Bassanio must be counted at first, is more able to praise her beauty and wealth than any virtue she might possess. In addition to that Bassanio shows an unfortunate lack of ability when it comes to handling money, which puts him into close connection with many of Elisabeth's courtiers. The trade monopolies given out by the Queen of England to her circle of admirers, the cultic revenue she received in return and her coquetry with power and love in foreign policy, are all assembled in the money-and-love theme of *The Merchant of Venice*. This mild mockery, however, is counterbalanced by Portia's solution of all problems in the last act:

Shakespeare's goal is [...] to rebind what had been torn asunder into a new unity, under aristocratic leadershipp. [622]

Furthermore, we must consider Portia's role of bringer of mercy and judgement in the trial scene, where she gets the chance to 'save' Shylocks life, and even his soul, while Elisabeth herself was confined to a kind of helplessness concerning Essex and his trial against Dr. Lopéz. Both women, however, act their part, filling a man's office, relying on their own judgement and arguing the law.

The play of *Macbeth* as issued under the rule of King James presents no problem concerning its political nature and reflects upon the pressing questions of succession, state violence, tyranny and the divine order, all brought to the public mind by the accession of James in 1603.

The fate of Macbeth presents the making of a tyrant and the dreadful consequences of his rule in the troubled realms of Scotland, presented here as the accurate blueprint of all English prejudices. However, the play also evokes the conviction that even a tyrant may start out with good intentions and reflects on the sad truth that good intentions alone are not fit to rule a kingdom. The outward

---

[622] Cohen, Walter; The Merchant of Venice *and the Possibilities of Historical Criticism*.; pp. 777

appearance and inward intentions of a ruler and the considerable discrepancy that may lie between these two is also brought to mind in this analysis for the first time and was directly reflected upon James' rule in England. The imperial charge that ruined Macbeth is here brought forth as a warning against the abuse of state violence and the confusion of holy order and royal prerogative. Yet in the meta-level prophecies of the witches, the union of England and Scotland is still palpable, though Macbeth tries to reach it via the wrong means. The health – mentally and bodily – of a king and its reflection on the body politic is most pronounced in this context, as nature itself rises against Macbeth's rule.

The play must therefore in a political context be considered as a critique of absolutistic rule, for it is too easily confused with tyranny. The inclusion of supernatural powers in these circumstances, however, are necessary – as has been shown – as a mark of the unnaturalness of Macbeth and a basis for his destruction, yet in a political way the witches 'help' is actually non-existent. The ruthless rooting out of opposition, the regicide and abuse of state power arise from the circle of cruelty, perverted justification and misled ambition enclosing Macbeth. The fight of good and evil is fought not against the witches, but within the person of the monarch itself. It is therefore just as well that James' actual 'ancestor' Banquo is excluded from this actions, as his line embodies the hope of a brighter future – and Shakespeare thus escapes the all too obvious reprimand of his king:

> *We must thus conclude that although Shakespeare did not hesitate to flatter King James by repeating the monarch's own pet ideas, he did so only when they did not conflict with his own convictions.*[623]

Still, the example of Macbeth should have alerted King James to the dark side of a king's prerogative, even while eluding direct accusation.

The questions of tyranny and prerogative, law and mercy are earlier taken up in *Measure for Measure* thus continuing – or rather foreshadowing – strands from both plays. Duke Vincentio again is not similar enough to King James to provide actual ground for an accusation of slander, yet it is conclusive enough to underline the results taken from the analysis of *Macbeth*. On the one hand, the fear

---

[623] Sinfield, Alan; Macbeth: history, ideology and intellectuals.; pp. 205

of rebellion and revolution is caught in the Duke's espionage on his people, but furthermore the divine mission, infallibility and holy justice are subtly questioned in the outcome of the trial scene.

The divine right proclaimed by the *Basilikon Doron* is in this play exercised through Duke Vincentio, who thus simply refrains from taking the blame for his lax use of the law and puts his deputy in the position of a scapegoat. Here again is the discrepancy of outward appearance and inward intention noticeable. Measure for Measure *suggests that the essential question that links politics and literature in the Jacobean period is representation.*[624]

The two bodies of the king, the holy and the common, are exemplified in Vincentio's disguise as friar and his reappearance in the last act, though to an ironic extent as his dislike for making a spectacle of himself is questionable in his staging of justice in the trial scene. This trial scene in addition shows again that good intentions are not enough to rule a kingdom, as the Duke's attempt at forcing justice just ends in forced marriages, and yet it also provides through its character's silences many possibilities to conceal this kind of criticism.

The infallibility of a divine ruler is thus cast into doubt again, as is the Duke's virtuous mystique in Lucio's slanders, for which he is as harshly punished as Raleigh had been in his trial. The absurd combination of shyness and pompousness observed in the Duke should of course be considered in the light of James' attempt at a staged justice in the Raleigh trial, as should his incapability to find trustworthy counsellors.

> *The Duke's role is carefully brought into question – although the Duke does not notice this, and perhaps James did not either.*[625]

The Duke's deputy Angelo serves in *Measure for Measure* as the blueprint of a Puritan hypocrite, even if Vincentio's assumed virtuousness is no better. The favouritism shown by Vincentio, his ignorance of Escalus' more tested suitability and his readiness to dispose of Angelo, once he fails, cast a very unfriendly light upon Vincentio's character, which unfortunately is mirrored by King James' treatment of his counsellors, as the fate of Robert Cecil exemplifies.

---

[624] Hawkes, Terence; *Take Me to Your Leda.*; pp. 239
[625] Hammond, Paul; *The Argument of* Measure for Measure.; pp. 516

The loyalty and ability of counsellors and favourites, however, remains a problem for King James and a subject for Shakespeare in *The Winter's Tale*. This play does, as did the *Merchant of Venice*, reflect some contemporary social developments, apart from its occupation with monarchy, but the main emphasis lies again with the development of tyranny out of prerogative, the question of succession and the questionability of trustworthy counsel.

The authority of the crown – the King's right to rule as he wished – was thus an issue of considerable importance in the years before Leontes' tyranny was depicted for Jacobean audiences.[626]

Leontes' unreason in both neglecting and accepting the advice offered to him, first by his courtiers and than by Paulina, reflect yet again the dangerous assumption of the infallibility of a divine monarch's justice.

Leontes' deliberately destabilizes his succession, endangers his kingdom and brings the forces of nature into disarray in the pursuit of his royal will, a move that is mirrored by his counterpart Polixenes. Only though the miracle of Perdita's return and Hermione's resurrection is a great catastrophe for both kingdoms avoided.

The problem of just rule and tyranny is also taken up by the resemblances of Hermione, Perdita, Catherine and Elisabeth. It would go too far to announce *The Winter's Tale* to be a reprimand for King Henry's breach with Rome in the consequences of Leontes' denial of the oracle.

Yet Henry, as England's 'last absolute monarch' would serve as a perfect example of how the royal prerogative can go wrong in its pursuit of an heir at all costs and its unscrupulous persecution of opposition. It should have struck James that history does not likely provide a miracle to wipe out errors and neither does Time normally step in to right a flawed justice.

---

[626] Kurland, Stuart M.; "We need no more of your advice": *Political Realism in* The Winter's Tale.; pp. 368

Subject of the Crown?

> *Shakespeare, notoriously, has a way of anticipating all possibilities.*[627]

It was the aim of this essay to elaborate the Tudor and Stuart sovereignty in Shakespeare's non-historical plays. It has hopefully become clear that such political allusions can be found frequently in his work and that he chose to involve references to contemporary monarchs in a more subtle way than a history play would have allowed, due to the control issued by the Stationers Office. What is more, the plays analysed in this essay show considerable similarities concerning their political nature. While *The Merchant of Venice*, written under Elisabeth's rule, is occupied with social change, suitorship and the relation of love, money and power, the plays performed for King James show a mutual attraction for questions of tyranny, succession, divine rule and favouritism.

Criticism and praise in all of those plays go almost hand in hand, blurring each other, contradicting each other, and oftentimes creating just the kind of ambiguity, which makes them 'problem-plays'. We can, however, conclude that – apart perhaps from the witch queen of *Macbeth* – the allusions to Queen Elisabeth are not that tinged with criticism as are the ones relating to King James. Her personifications of Portia and Perdita may be arrogant at times, mocking, coquettish or, in Perdita's case, ill-disposed against the theatre. Yet they still are the bringers of peace, the virgin goddesses of harmony and mercy.

Figures like Macbeth, Vincentio or even Leontes, in their persistence on royal prerogative, divine rule and frequent abuse of state power, are much more questionable. Shakespeare's depictions of sovereigns in these cases may be realistic to the edge of slandering. He exposes Elisabeth's all but promiscuous flirting with her opportunistic 'suitors', as he exposes James hypocrisy in proclaiming virtues he himself does not pursue. The infallibility of a monarch is subtly neglected in all analysed plays, as are the holy missions of justice and mystical powers of a monarch's rule. As has been elaborated already in the analysis of *Measure for Measure*, Shakespeare puts his sovereigns into a position from where they can be judged by

---
[627] Sinfield, Alan; Macbeth: *history, ideology and intellectuals*.; pp. 74

common sense, reducing them to their limited human existence and taking away the hypocritical garments of godly power. A fairy tale miracle like in *The Winter's Tale* does thus not enhance the king's mystique in Shakespeare's 'universe', but diminishes it. Yet a trace of anti-royalist feeling of the pre-civil-war period can not be justifiably found in Shakespeare's descriptions of monarchy, as the claim that monarchy is not infallible does certainly not mean that monarchy is useless or that it should be erased. To strip a monarch of this alleged 'pharaonic' god-king status, which is palpable in both Elisabeth's cult of the virgin goddess and in James' holy mission does not leave him powerless.

In fact Shakespeare seems to suggest that a more realistic self-esteem and a more clear sighted evaluation of a monarchs flaws and virtues would in fact advance the possibilities of the body politic. The atmosphere of the plays does moreover suggest that a king, who accepts his human limitations and surrenders to the possibility of false judgement becomes more human and in consequence more able to pursue the necessary business of realpoilitk, even if humanity is limited compared to godly powers.

Annex

Seventeenth century print of the members of the Gunpowder plot being hanged, drawn and quartered.

Bibliography

Primary Sources

Shakespeare, William. 1993. *The Merchant of Venice.* Cambridge: Cambridge Univ. Press.

Shakespeare, William. 2007. *Macbeth.* Cambridge: Cambridge Univ. Press.

Shakespeare, William. 2007 [updated ed.]. *Measure for Measure.* Cambridge: Cambridge Univ. Press.

Shakespeare, William. 2007. *The Winter's Tale.* Cambridge: Cambridge Univ. Press.

Secondary Sources

Alexander, Catherine M. S. 2004. "Introduction." In: Alexander, Catherine M. S. (ed.), *Shakespeare and Politics.* Cambridge: Cambridge Univ. Press.

Badawi, M. M. 1981. *Background to Shakespeare.* London: Macmillan Press.

Baker, Elliot. 1995. "The Queens Hand in the *Merchant of Venice.*" In: Goldstein, Gary B. (ed.). *The Elizabethan Review.* Middle Village, NY: Goldstein Press, Vol. 3. pp.21-31.

Barrol, Leeds. 1991. *Politics, Plague and Shakespeare's Theatre. The Stuart Years.* Ithaca & London: Cornell University Press.

Benston, Alice N. 1979. "Portia, the Law and the Tripatite Structure Of the *Merchant of Venice.*" In: Shakespeare Association of America. *Shakespeare Quarterly.* Washington D.C.: Folger Shakespeare Library, Vol. 30. pp. 367-385.

Bennett, Alexandra G. 2006. "Testifiying in the Court of Public Opinion: Margaret Cavendish Reworks *The Winter's Tale.*" In: Romack, Katherine; Fitzmaurice, James (eds.). *Cavendish and Shakespeare, Interconnections.* Aldershot: Ashgate Publishing Company. pp. 85-102.

Bernthal, Craig A. 1992. "Staging Justice: James I. and the Trial Scenes of *Measure for Measure.*" In: Patten, Robert L.(ed.). *Studies in English*

Literature 1500-1900. Houston, Texas: Johns Hopkins University Press. Vol. 32. pp. 247-269.

Bloom, Allan. 1964. *Shakespeare's Politics.* Chicago: Univ. of Chicago Press.

Bradbook, Muriel. 1994 [rev. ed.]. "The Origins of *Macbeth.*" In: Wain, John (ed.). *Shakespeare* Macbeth. *A Casebook.* Houndmills: Macmillan. pp. 236-258.

Bradley, A. C. 1994 [rev. ed.]. "*Macbeth.*" In: Wain, John (ed.). *Shakespeare* Macbeth. *A Casebook.* Houndmills: Macmillan. pp.105-139.

Braunmueller, A.R. 2007. "Introduction" In: Braunmueller, A.R. (ed.). *Shakespeare, William; Macbeth; New Cambridge Shakespeare Ed.* Cambridge: Cambridge Univ. Press.

Brown, Carolyn E. 1996. "Duke Vincentio of *Measure for Measure* and *King James I.* of England: The Poorest Princes in Christendom." In: Clio; Clio-Institute University of Wisconsin Bloomington: Indiana Univ. Press, Vol. 26, pp. 51-78.

Calhoun, Howell V. 1942. "James I. And the Witch Scenes in *Macbeth.*" In: The Shakespeare Association of America. *The Shakespeare Association Bulletin.* New York, NY: Folger Shakespeare Library, Vol. 17. pp. 184-189.

Cerasano, S. pp. (ed.). 2004. *William Shakespeare's* The Merchant of Venice. *A Sourcebook.* London: Routledge.

Cohen, Walter. 1982. "*The Merchant of Venice* and the Possibilities of Historical Criticism." In: Ferguson, Frances (ed.). *English Literary History.* Baltimore, Maryland: Johns Hopkins Univ. Press, Vol. 49. pp. 765-785.

Coyle, Martin. 2001. "Shakespeare: Theatrical and Historical Contexts." In: Rylance, Rick; Simons, Judy (eds.). *Literature in Context.* Houndmills: Palgrave. pp.15-33.

Draper, John W. 1937-38. "*Macbeth* as a Compliment to *James I.*" In: Hoops, Johannes (ed.). *Englische Studien. Organ für englische Philologie unter Mitberücksichtigung des englischen Unterrichts auf höheren Stufen.* New York, NY: Johnson Reprint. Vol. 72. pp. 207-221.

Dunkel, Wilbur. 1962. "Law and Equity in *Measure for Measure.*" In: Shakespeare Association of America. *Shakespeare Quarterly.* Washington D.C.: Folger Shakespeare Library, Vol. 13. pp. 275-285.

Esser, Raingard. 2004. *Die Tudors und die Stuarts.* Stuttgart: Kohlhammer Urban.

Gash, Anthony. 1998. "Shakespeare's Carnival and the Sacred: *The Winter's Tale* and *Measure for Measure.*" In: Knowles, Roland (ed.). *Shakespeare in Carnival.* Houndmill: Macmillan Press. pp.177-211.

Geisen, Herbert. 2000. „Nachwort." In: Geisen, Herbert (ed.). *Shakespeare, William; The Winter's Tale; Zweisprachige Ausgabe.* Stuttgart: Reclam.

Gibbons, Brian. 2007 [updated ed.]. "Introduction." In: Gibbons, Brian (ed.). *Shakespeare, William; Measure for Measure; New Cambridge Shakespeare Ed.* Cambridge: Cambridge Univ. Press.

Goldberg, Jonathan. 1989. *James I. and the Politics of Literature.* Stanford, CA: Stanford Univ. Press.

Goldstein, Gary B. 2004. "Did Queen Elisabeth Use the Theatre for Social and Political Propaganda?" In: The Shakespeare-Oxford Society. *The Oxfordian.* Port Washington: Kennikat Press; Vol. 7. pp. 153-169.

Grene, David. 1967. *Reality and the Heroic Pattern. Last Plays of Ibsen, Shakespeare, and Sophocles.* London: Univ. of Chicago Press. pp. 68-86.

Hammond, Paul. 1986. "The Argument of *Measure for Measure.*" In: The Massachusetts Center for Renaissance Studies. *English Literary Renaissance.* Oxford: Blackwell, Vol. 16. pp. 496-519.

Hardman, C. B. 1994. "Shakespeare's *Winter's Tale* and the Stuart Golden Age." In: Bradshaw, David (ed.). *The Review of English Studies.* Oxford: Oxford Univ. Press, Vol. 45. pp. 221-229.

Hawkes, Terence. 2004. "Take Me to Your Leda." In: Alexander, Catherine M. S. (ed.). *Shakespeare and Politics.* Cambridge: Cambridge Univ. Press. pp. 219-236.

Heilman, Robert B. 1977. "The Criminal as Tragic Hero: Dramatic Methods." In: *Aspects of Macbeth. Articles Reprinted from* Shakespeare Survey. Cambridge: Cambridge Univ. Press. pp.26-39.

Höfele, Andreas. 1997. "The Great Image of Authority. Königsbilder in Shakespeare's Theatre." In: Deutsche Shakespeare-Gesellschaft. *Shakespeare Jahrbuch*. Bochum: Kamp Verlag, Vol. 133. pp. 77-98.

Horton, Craig. 2003. "...the country must diminish: Jacobean London and the Production of Pastoral Space in *The Winter's Tale*." In: Australian & New Zealand Association for Medieval and Early Modern Studies. *Parergon*. Canberra: Univ. of West. Australia Press, Vol. 20. pp. 85-107.

Howard, Herbert. 1965. "Shakespeare's Flattery in *Measure for Measure*." In: Shakespeare Association of America. *Shakespeare Quarterly*. Washington D.C.: Folger Shakespeare Library, Vol. 16. pp. 29-37.

Jack, Jane H. 1955. "*Macbeth, King James* and the *Bible*." In: Norris, Edward T. (ed.). *English Literary History*. Baltimore, Maryland: Johns Hopkins Univ. Press, Vol. 22. pp. 173-193.

Jensen, Phebe. 2004. "Singing Psalms to Horn-Pipes: Festivity, Iconoclasm and Chatholicism in *The Winter's Tale*." In: Shakespeare Association of America. *Shakespeare Quarterly*. Washington D.C.: Folger Shakespeare Library, Vol. 55. pp. 279-306.

Joughin, John J. 2004. "Shakespeare and Politics: An Introduction." In: Alexander, Catherine M. S. (ed.). *Shakespeare and Politics*. Cambridge: Cambridge Univ. Press. pp.1-22.

Kenyon, J. pp. 1958. *The Stuarts. A Study in English Kingshipp*. London & Glasgow: Collins Clear-Type Press.

Kinney, Arthur F. 1991. "Shakespeare's *Macbeth* and the Question of Nationalism." In: Newey, Vincent (ed.). *Literature and Nationalism*. Liverpool: Liverpool Univ. Press. pp. 56-76.

Kinney, Arthur F. 1993. "Scottish History, the Union of the Crowns, and The Issue of Right Rule: The Case of Shakespeare's *Macbeth*." In: Brink, Jean R.; Gentrup, William F. (eds.). *Renaissance Culture in Context: Theory and Practice*. Aldershot: Scolar Press. pp.18-53.

Klause, John. 2003. "Catholic and Protestant, Jesuit and Jew: Historical Religion in *The Merchant of Venice*." In: Taylor, Denis; Beauregard, David N. (eds.). *Shakespeare and the Culture of Christianity in Early Modern England*. New York, NY: Fordham Upp. pp. 180-221.

Kurland, Stuart M. 1991. "We need no more of your advice: Political Realism in *The Winter's Tale*." In: Patten, Robert L.(ed.). *Studies in English Literature 1500-1900*. Houston, Texas: Johns Hopkins University Press, Vol. 31. pp. 365-381.

Lancashire, Anne. 1991. "Recent Studies in Elizabethan and Jacobean Drama." In: Patten, Robert L.(ed.). *Studies in English Literature 1500-1900*. Houston, Texas: Johns Hopkins University Press, Vol. 31. pp. 385-421.

Landau, Aaron. 2003. "No settled senses of the world can match the pleasure of that madness: The Politics of Unreason in The Winter's Tale." In: Institut de Recherches sur la Renaissance, l'Âge Classique et les Lumières. *Cahiers Élisabéthains*. Montpellier: A Biannual Journal of English Renaissance Studies. Univ. of Montpellier Press, Vol. 64. pp. 29-42.

Lechter-Siegel, Amy. 1992. "Isabella's Silence: The Consolidation of Power in Measure for Measure." In: Di Cesare, Mario A. (ed.). *Reconsidering the Renaissance*. Binghamton, N.Y.: Medieval and Renaissance Texts and Studies Press; Vol. 33. pp. 371-80.

Marcus, Leah S. 1992. "Recent Studies in Elizabethan and Jacobean Drama." In: Patten, Robert L.(ed.). *Studies in English Literature 1500-1900*. Houston, Texas: Johns Hopkins University Press, Vol. 32. pp. 361-401.

Mahler, Andreas. 2002. *Shakespeare's Subkulturen. Typen, Tricks, Topographien*. Passau: Stutz Verlag.
Mahood, M. M. 1993. "Introduction." In: Mahood, M.M. (ed.). *Shakespeare, William; The Merchant of Venice; New Cambridge Shakespeare Ed*. Cambridge: Cambridge Univ. Press.

Maurer, Michael. 1997. *Eine kleine Geschichte Englands*. Stuttgart: Reclam.

McCoy, Richard C. 1989. "Thou Idol Ceremony: Elisabeth I., The Henriad, and the Rites of the English Monarchy." In: Zimmerman, Susan; Weissman, Ronald F. E. (eds.). *Urban Life in the Renaissance*. Cranbury, NJ: Associated University Presses. pp. 240-68.

Miles, Rosalind. 1976. *The Problem of Measure for Measure. A Historical Investigation*. London: Vision Press.

Moody, A. D. 1981 [4th repr.]. *Shakespeare. The Merchant of Venice.* London: Arnold Ldt.

Moran, Andrew Damian. 2004. "The Chapel and the Gallery: Religion and Theatre in *The Winter's Tale.*" In: University Microfilms International. *Dissertation Abstracts International / A, The Humaniaties and Social Sciences.* Ann Arbor, Mich: UMI, Vol. 64. pp. 2501.

Muir, Kenneth. 1977. "Image and Symbol in *Macbeth.*" In: *Aspects of Macbeth. Articles Reprinted from Shakespeare Survey.* Cambridge: Cambridge Univ. Press. pp. 66-76.

Newman, Karen. 2004. "Portia's Ring: Unruly Women and Structures of Exchange in *The Merchant of Venice.*" In: Cerasano, S. pp. (ed.). *William Shakespeare's The Merchant of Venice. A Sourcebook.* London: Routledge. pp. 84-86.

O'Harae, Alison. 2003. "Which Model? Whose Measure?: Sexuality, Morality and Power in *Measure for Measure* and *Basilicon Doron.*" In: Chowdhury, Radhiah (ed.). *Philament Free Journal of Postgraduate Scholarshipp.* Vol. 1.

Pache, Walter. 2004. "Nachwort." In: Pache, Walter (ed.). *Shakespeare, William; Measure for Measure.* Stuttgart: Reclam.

Puschmann-Nalenz, Barbara. 2006. "Nachwort." In: Puschmann-Nalenz, Barbara (ed.). *Shakespeare, William; The Merchant of Venice.* Stuttgart: Reclam.

Rex, Richard. 2006. *Die Tudors. Englands Aufbruch in die Neuzeit 1485-1603.* Essen: Magnus.

Ribner, Irving. 1953. "Political Doctrine in *Macbeth.*" In: Shakespeare Association of America.
Shakespeare Quarterly. Washington D.C.: Folger Shakespeare Library, Vol. 4. pp.202-206.

Rohjan-Deyk, Barbara. 1996. "Nachwort." In: Rohjan-Deyk, Barbara (ed.). *Shakespeare, William; Macbeth.* Stuttgart: Reclam.

Rutledge, Douglas F. 1988. "The Structural Parallel Between Rituals of Reversal, Jacobean Political Theory, and *Measure for Measure.*" In: Iowa

State University of Science and Technology. *Iowa State Journal of Research.* Ames, Iowa: Iowa State Univ. Press; Vol. 62. pp. 421-441.

Siegel, pp. N. 1953. "*Measure for Measure*: The Significance of the Title." In: Shakespeare Association of America. *Shakespeare Quarterly.* Washington D.C.: Folger Shakespeare Library, Vol. 4. pp.317-321.

Sinfield, Alan. 1986. "*Macbeth*: history, ideology and intellectuals." In: MacCabe, Colin (ed.). *Critical Quarterly.* Ames, IA: Blackwell, Vol. 28. pp. 63-77.

Skura, Meredith Anne. 2000. "Recent Studies in Tudor and Stuart Drama." In: Patten, Robert L.(ed.). *Studies in English Literature 1500-1900.* Houston, Texas: Johns Hopkins University Press, Vol. 40. pp. 355-389.

Smith, Peter J. 1998. "Characterization and Stereotype: Theatrical Convention in *The Merchant of Venice.*" In: Lascombes, André (ed.). *Tudor Theatre: Let There Be Covenents....* Bern: Peter Lang. pp. 255-270.

Snyder, Susan. 2007. "Introduction." In: Snyder, Susan (ed.). *Shakespeare, William; The Winter's Tale; New Cambridge Shakespeare Ed.* Cambridge: Cambridge Univ. Press.

Stevenson, David L. 1959. "The Role of James I. in Shakespeare's *Measure for Measure.*" In: Allen, Don Cameron (ed.). *English Literary History* Baltimore, Maryland: Johns Hopkins Univ. Press, Vol. 26. pp. 188-209.

Steele, Mary Susan. 1968 [repr.]. *Plays & Masques at Court During the Reigns of Elisabeth, James and Charles.* New York: Russel&Russel.

Stirling, Brents. 1953. "The Unity of *Macbeth.*" In: Shakespeare Association of America. *Shakespeare Quarterly.* Washington D.C.: Folger Shakespeare Library, Vol. 4. pp.385-395.

Suerbaum, Ulrich. 1989. *Das elisabethanische Zeitalter.* Stuttgart: Reclam.

Tebbetts, Terrell L. 1985. "Talking Back to the King: *Measure for Measure* and the *Basilikon Doron.*" In: West Chester State College Special Funds Office. *College Literature.* West Chester, Pa.: West Chester Univ. Press, Vol. 12. pp. 122-134.

Tiffany, Grace. 1996. "*Macbeth*, Paternity and the Anglicization of James I." In: Indiana University of Pennsylvania Faculty of Humanities. *Studies in the Humanities*. Bloomington: Indiana Univ. Press, Vol. 32. pp. 148-162.

Vanita, Ruth. 2000. "Mariological Memory in *The Winter's Tale* and *Henry VIII*." In: Patten, Robert L.(ed.). *Studies in English Literature 1500-1900*. Houston, Texas: Johns Hopkins University Press, Vol. 40. pp. 311-337.

Wasson, John. 1970. "*Measure for Measure*: A Text for Court Performance?." In: Shakespeare Association of America. *Shakespeare Quarterly*. Washington D.C.: Folger Shakespeare Library, Vol. 21. pp. 17-24.

Williams, George Walton. 1982. "*Macbeth*: King James's Play." In: Roudané, Matthew C. (ed.). *South Atlantic Review*. Tuscaloosa, ALA. Georgia State Univ. Press, Vol. 47. pp. 12-21.

Williamson, James A. 1953. *The Tudor Golden Age*. London: Longmans Green.

Wilson, Richard. 2007. "Blood Will Have Blood: Regime Change in *Macbeth*." In: Deutsche Shakespeare-Gesellschaft. *Shakespeare Jahrbuch*. Bochum: Kamp Verlag, Vol. 143. pp. 11-35.

Wilson, Richard. 2002. "Shakespeare in Hate. Performing the Virgin Queen." In: *Poetica. Schriften zur Literaturwissenschaft*. München: Wilhelm Fink Verlag, Vol. 34. pp. 149-167.

Worden, Blair. 2004. "Shakespeare and Politics." In: Alexander, Catherine M. S. (ed.). *Shakespeare and Politics*. Cambridge: Cambridge Univ. Press. pp. 22-44.

Wortham, Christopher. 1996. "Shakespeare, James I. and the Matter of Britain." In: Barry, Peter; Newton, Ken (eds.). *English. The Journal of the English Association*. Bangor, Wales: Bangor Univ. Press, Vol. 45. pp. 97-121.

Zurcher, Amelia. 2003. "Untimely Monuments: Stoicism, History, and the Problem of Utility in The Winter's Tale." In: Ferguson, Frances (ed.). *English Literary History*. Baltimore, Maryland: Johns Hopkins Univ. Press, Vol. 70. pp. 903-925.

Andere Veröffentlichungen

Manuela Sonntag - B(r)uchstücke (Anthologie)

Für den Leser – und auch manchmal für den Autor – ist eine Kurzgeschichte e Fenster in eine größere Erzählung. Ein helles Spotlight, das nur einen kleine Teil eines Lebens, einer Handlung oder einer Idee beleuchtet und den große Kontext im Dunklen lässt.
Wenn wir eine Kurzgeschichten-Sammlung lesen, schlendern wir also ein bunte Schaufensterpassage entlang - hinter jedem dünnen Glas eine neue Ide ein neues Bild, eine neue Geschichte, von der jede das Potenzial in sich trage könnte eine große, eigenständige Saga zu werden.

Christine Schuhmann & Manuela Sonntag - Perlen für die Säue (Anthologie)

In unseren unbescholtenen Schuljahren – Rund um die erste aufsehenerregende Pisastudie - hat man einmal zu uns gesagt: ‚Romane mögen ja noch angehen, aber Kurzgeschichten und Gedichte für deutsche Jugendliche unter 25 schreiben, dass ist Perlen vor die Säue werfen.'
Gut, haben wir uns damals gedacht, dann ist es genau das, was wir tun wollen. ‚Perlen FÜR die Säue' schreiben und zeigen, dass deutsche Jugend mitnichten so tumb und unreflektiert ist, wie man sie gerne sehen möchte.
Und wenn wir alles richtig gemacht haben, dann ist es auch geeignet für Menschen, die sich vielleicht zum erstem Mal hinsetzen und endlich aufschreiben, was ihnen schon lange im Kopf herumgeht, weil sie uns einfach glauben, dass Sprache und Literatur Spaß machen können, wenn man es einfach mal versucht!

Manuela Sonntag - William Shakespeare, Subject of the Crown? (Sachbuch)

Shakespeare and his work have inspired many books by literary scholars and historians throughout the centur Yet the problem stated above has been an essential part in all of them. What can we know about a man of who nothing is known, except what he chose to let his characters say and do? Can there really be any certainty abo Shakespeare's opinions, thoughts, ideas, even on the most trivial matters? Isn't this a dangerous confusion person and fiction?
This essay will not try to find certainty among the many statements made about author and work over the yea but try to relate some of Shakespeare's 'non-historical' plays to contemporary politics – one part dedicated the English Renaissance as a century of change and progress, the other part literary analysis of Shakespe are's plays with consideration of this political zeitgeist.

Andere Veröffentlichungen

Manuela Sonntag - Der Rosenfriedhof (Roman)

Wir alle sind ständig auf der Suche.
Auf der Suche nach Glück, Liebe, Geld, Macht oder dem Sinn unseres Lebens. Rebecca Curtis ist da keine Ausnahme.
Obwohl ihr Leben eine Blaupause für amerikanisches Familienglück zu sein scheint, kann sie den Verlust ihrer ersten großen Liebe nicht akzeptieren. Doch als sie beginnt sich mit dem Sinn ihres Lebens auseinanderzusetzen, führt sie die Suche nicht nur in ein unbekanntes Land, sondern schickt sie auch auf eine Reise in die Vergangenheit, die ihr bisheriges Leben völlig auf den Kopf stellt.
Mitten in den grünen Hügeln Irlands begegnet sie Hass und Liebe, Intrigen, Mord, Freundschaft und Erfüllung und muss lernen, dass manchmal nur der weiteste Weg zu uns selbst führt.

Manuela Sonntag - Krieg den Schatten (Roman)
Veröffentlichung voraussichtlich 2017

Am Anfang waren der Himmel und die Sterne und sie waren unendlich und uralt. Doch eines Tages wurde die Göttin Gaya geboren und sie beschloss, dass es eine Welt geben müsse, in dem Feuer und Wasser, Wind und Erde existieren müssten, denn alles was der Himmel und die Sterne ihr bieten konnten, waren Licht und Dunkelheit."
Elysion ist ein Kontinent im Gleichgewicht von Licht und Schatten. Im Lichtreich wachen die Steinweisen über den Frieden und die Priesterschaft verehrt die Geister der Elemente.
Im Schattenreich herrschen die Jormundr über die mächtigen Familien der dunklen Völker.
Seit Jahrtausenden hielten sich diese Kräfte gegenseitig in Balance. Jetzt muss sich diese Welt verändern.
Eine ungewöhnliche Apparatur, ein wilder Drache, ein undenkbarer Krieg gegen die Schatten und eine unvorhergesehene Liebesgeschichte wird sie dazu zwingen.

Thomas Michalski

Thomas Michalski wurde 1983 in Euskirchen geboren und wuchs anschließend in der kleinen Stadt Schleiden in der Eifel auf. 2003 zog er nach Aachen und absolvierte dort an der RWTH ein Studium der Germanistischen und Allgemeinen Literaturwissenschaft sowie der Philosophie.
Er lebt weiterhin in Aachen und arbeitet dort als Layouter und Grafiker.

Er war mehrere Jahre als Journalist tätig, veröffentlicht Artikel in verschiedenen Fachmagazinen und ist der Autor mehrerer Bücher aus den Bereichen Sachbuch und Belletristik.

Weitere Informationen unter www.thomas-michalski.de

🐦 @seelenworte

Einfach Filme machen
Zweite Auflage

Erscheint 2016/2017

Jeder kann Filme machen!

Man braucht dafür keine Multi-Millionen-Dollar-Budgets, keine aufwendigen Spezialeffekt-Werkstätten oder weltberühmte Stars. Was man braucht ist vor allem eine spannende Idee, eine Kamera und etwas Kreativität.
Das nötige Hintergrundwissen hingegen findet man in diesem Buch. Vom Schreiben des Drehbuchs und Planen der Drehtage, vom Suchen und Finden von Crew und Schauspielern, über Equipment, Inszenierung, Schnitt und Spezialeffekte bis hin zum Marketing verrät einem Einfach Filme machen alles, was man wissen muss.
Hier werden professionelle Theorie mit Tipps und Tricks aus Jahren des No-Budget-Filmens vereint wie es bisher noch nie geschehen ist.

Die Erstauflage des Buches erschien 2009. In der komplett überarbeiteten zweiten Auflage werden technische Entwicklungen seither berücksichtigt und zahlreiche Themengebiete noch weiter vertieft.

Lovecraft und Duve
8,95 Euro

ISBN:
978-3-732-27348-5

H.P. Lovecraft und Karen Duve – zwei Schriftsteller, die auf den ersten Blick keinerlei Parallelen zueinander aufzuweisen scheinen. Der eine einer der Begründer der modernen, amerikanischen Schauerliteratur, die andere eines der Aushängeschilder der Bewegung, die als deutsches „Fräuleinwunder" tituliert für junge Autorinnen um die Jahrtausendwende stand.
Als Duve zur Welt kam, war Lovecraft bereits 24 Jahre verstorben.

Und doch finden sich in Texten der beiden Autoren Parallelen. Lovecraft wie Duve verwenden in einigen ihrer bekanntesten Texte das Motiv humanoider Fisch-Mensch-Hybriden; doch wo formale Ähnlichkeit herrscht, findet sich zugleich große, inhaltliche Differenz.
Doch wie kommt es dazu? Warum ist dieses in sich eigenwillige Motiv so einprägsam, und doch zugleich so offen, dass es grundverschiedenen Schriftstellern mit fast diametralen Ansichten dennoch gleichermaßen dienen kann.

Dieses Buch begibt sich auf die Suche nach einer Antwort.

Dunkle, schauerliche Wälder und geheimnisvolle, im Nebel verborgene Moore – die Eifel kann ein sehr gruseliger Ort sein. Das merken auch immer wieder Fremde, die sich in diese kalte und regnerische Region wagen.

In „Das Dorfgeheimnis" ist es ein junger Mann, der eigentlich einen Freund besuchen möchte, doch als er diesen nicht antrifft, auf die Spur eines grässlichen, weit in die Geschichte eines Eifeldorfes reichenden Geheimnisses stößt.

In „Verfluchte Eifel" machen sich fünf Studenten auf in die Region, um einerseits Urlaub zu machen, andererseits aber auch, um einer alten Legende um einen mysteriösen Kirchenraub nachzugehen. Doch nicht nur geraten sie so einigen örtlichen Verbrechern in die Quere, auch an der Legende scheint mehr dran zu sein, als den jungen Leuten lieb sein kann.

Verfluchte Eifel
8,95 Euro

ISBN:
978-3-7392-1874-8

Als eine junge Frau tot in einer Hütte im Wald aufgefunden wird, scheint die Liste offener Fragen kaum ein Ende zu nehmen: Wer ist sie? Warum liegt sie dort im Wald? Wer hat sie ermordet – und warum?

Journalist Philipp Kreil kann sich mit der offiziellen Erklärung, es sei eine willkürliche Tat gewesen, nicht zufrieden geben. Gemeinsam mit seiner jungen Kollegin Karin beginnt er eigene Nachforschungen. Die Spuren führen sie zur ansässigen Universität – gibt es in den Mauern ihrer Alma Mater ein Geheimnis, das einen Mord wert ist?

Schleier aus Schnee
11 Euro

ISBN:
978-3-7386-5966-5

Jedes Jahr pilgern die Leute aus dem ganzen Umland in ein kleines Eifeldorf, um einem ganz besonderen Osterritus beizuwohnen: Große Räder aus Holz werden mit Stroh und Reisig versehen, entfacht und eine kleine Steilklippe nahe der Siedlung hinabgeschickt, um die bösen Geister zu vertreiben. Ein Brauch, vielleicht so alt wie das Dorf selbst.

Als jedoch der ansässige Pfarrer während der Karfreitagsprozession ums Leben kommt, gerät das ganze Fest aus den Fugen. Weder der junge, vor kurzem erst zugezogene Bürgermeister, noch eine Journalistin, die eigentlich nur für einen Brauchtumsbericht angereist ist, können sich auf die Vorgänge einen Reim machen.

Als jedoch schon am Tag nach dem Mord ein Ersatz für den verstorbenen Priester eintrifft, direkt aus der Heiligen Stadt, wie man sagt, ist den beiden eines klar: Hier geht es um mehr, als es zunächst den Anschein hat

Verdorbene Asche
Erscheint 2016/17